HOW TO LEAVE THE MORMON CHURCH

An Exmormon's Guide to Rebuilding After Religion

ALYSSA GRENFELL

For privacy reasons, some names, locations, and dates may have been changed.

Title: How to Leave the Mormon Church: An Exmormon's Guide to Rebuilding After Religion

Edited by Jack Despain Zhou

Book and Cover Design by London J. Reid

Illustrations by Alyssa Grenfell

First Edition, 2023

Printed in the United States of America

Hardcover ISBN: 979-8-9893105-0-0
Paperback ISBN: 979-8-9893105-1-7
eBook ISBN: 979-8-9893105-2-4

@alyssadgrenfell

www.howtoleavethemormonchurch.com

To my husband, Jackson,
for epitomizing love
that transcends the confines of dogma

And to my sons, Eli and Westbrook,
this book is for you
I'm proud you'll never need to read it

CONTENTS

PART TWO

FOREWORD

It was 2001. I was a thirty-two-year-old Mormon father of three working for Microsoft in Redmond, Washington. My mind was pulled in a thousand directions as I balanced marriage, fatherhood, work, and church responsibilities. That summer, I was called by my bishop to teach early morning seminary. In the following months, I woke up every workday at 5 a.m. and carefully prepared to teach local high school students the basics of Mormon doctrine, history, and theology.

My family belonged to the Mormon church for six generations. As a devout member, I faithfully followed the Mormon path to become more like Jesus Christ. I went through four years of early morning high school seminary. During my two-year full-time LDS mission, I recruited over one hundred people into Mormonism. As a young adult, I spent almost five years at Brigham Young University taking numerous religion classes. After graduation, I married my wife, Margi, in the Washington D.C. Temple.

All this time spent dedicated to the church convinced me that if anyone knew Mormon history, doctrine, and theology—it was me. "I can teach this stuff in my sleep!" I confidently thought and enthusiastically accepted the bishop's call to teach seminary.

In the back of my mind, however, I knew I had a blind spot regarding church history. I had vague notions about Mormon polygamy and that my grandmother Karma was the daughter of a 3rd polygamous wife. I knew the Mormon church had denied priesthood and temple blessings to Black members before 1978, which never sat well with me. I was dimly aware that questions of historical and scientific validity swirled around the Book of Mormon—and the Bible, for that matter. But despite my lifelong commitment to Mormonism, my understanding of these issues was surprisingly thin.

With this awareness, I became even more committed to succeeding in my new calling. Teaching seminary would allow me to delve deeper into Mormon history, ultimately leading to an even stronger testimony of the church's foundational truth claims.

To my eventual shock and horror, my intensive investigation into church history had the opposite effect—leading to a total loss of my Mormon faith. Each time I discovered a troubling fact, I dug further, expecting to find information to resolve my concern. Instead, I slowly began to comprehend the depth of Mormonism's dark and troubled past.

In addition to the issues I was already familiar with, I discovered a mountain of profoundly troubling information about Joseph Smith. In all my years as a devout member, I had not heard these issues raised once. This included Joseph Smith's use of a peep stone in a hat to illegally dig for "buried treasure" and to "translate" the Book of Mormon. It included Joseph's pursuit and success in marrying fourteen-year-old girls. I could barely absorb the fact that he married women who were already married to other men, known as polyandry. I spent hours studying his faulty translation of the Book of Abraham.

As my faith evaporated, I began to feel overwhelmed and depressed. Halfway into my second year as a seminary teacher, I realized that I could no longer, in good faith, indoctrinate these teenagers in the same way that I had been indoctrinated. I resigned in embarrassment.

Spiraling into depressive shame, I began to realize how much of my life was built, utterly and unconditionally, around the church. My identity. My morality. Who I married. When I married. The size of my family. My friendships. My community. My career. My understanding of life, death, and the afterlife. Every aspect of my life was inextricably linked to my belief in the Mormon church. These foundational pillars disintegrated in an instant. It felt as though my soul died a thousand deaths in a way that only those who have grown up in a high-demand religion can adequately comprehend.

I was Truman in the Truman Show. I was Neo in The Matrix. I was Rapunzel in Tangled. I had been intentionally misled to believe in a reality that did not exist. And I felt utterly lost.

In the wake of my testimony collapse, I tried desperately to find support. I first went to my wife, Margi, with my concerns and discoveries. After she read some of the same Mormon history books, she immediately lost her belief in the church. Now, we were *both* at a loss for what to do next. Nearly all of our extended family were devout members of the church and surely would not look kindly on our "falling away." More significantly, we had spent the previous decade raising our three young children in the church, and they loved it as much as we did.

With tears streaming down her face, Margi asked me, "Well... what do *you* want to do?"

I had no clue.

In desperation, I went to my brother Joel. He was a faithful Mormon at the time and is one of the smartest and kindest humans I know. While I don't recall his exact words, he essentially said, "I don't want to talk about this, bro. I'm sure your issues are legitimate, but digging into this will only cause significant disruption in my life, especially in my marriage. I'm happier not knowing. I'm sorry, I can't help you."

Discouraged but undaunted, I sought advice from my Mormon bishop and stake president, who seemed stunned and could only offer platitudes. The Mormon church seemed to be either unaware of or utterly indifferent to this suffering.

Finally, I turned to my Mormon colleagues at Microsoft. Some wanted to lecture me about my faithlessness or ignore my concerns completely. Surprisingly, others were in a similar position as me but were terrified to reveal their loss of faith to their family and friends—spouses and parents included. I witnessed firsthand how silence and suppression around LDS disaffection contributed to depression, anxiety, addiction, divorce, and, at times, even suicidality. I saw others metaphorically blow up their lives and relationships as they left the church in unbridled anger.

I knew something needed to be done.

After struggling with depression and loneliness for a few more years, I decided to leave my lucrative job at Microsoft and spend the remainder of my life dedicated to supporting individuals in a faith crisis. In 2005, I started the Mormon Stories Podcast. The last twenty years of my life have been dedicated to exploring the complexities, problems, and gifts of the Mormon faith crisis through long-form personal stories.

In 2015, I completed a Ph.D. in Clinical and Counseling Psychology with an emphasis in supporting Mormons in religious faith transition. From there, I began hosting faith crisis workshops and retreats. In total, it is safe to say that I have personally counseled tens of thousands of Mormons who are either in the middle of a faith crisis or who have left the church entirely.

The pain, costs, and complexities of leaving a high-demand religion like Mormonism, Scientology, Jehovah's Witnesses, and Ultra-Orthodox Judaism are very real. For 20 years, I have personally witnessed highly alarming levels of depression and anxiety in those who lose their faith. Divorce, familial shunning, and even estrangement are far too common in a Mormon context. Many struggle with suicidality after losing faith.

That is precisely what makes this book so important.

As I have gotten to know Alyssa, I have been impressed by the depth and perspective she brings to the conversation. This book is an essential companion for those who feel lost, alone, and confused once their Mormon shelf breaks. Frankly, it is the resource *I so desperately needed* in the days, months, and years after my own loss of faith.

Alyssa comes from an orthodox Mormon background. Her LDS family is devout and includes prominent church officers. She had never tried coffee or watched an R-rated movie before her faith crisis. She served a full-time mission, and after returning home from her mission, she trained other missionaries at the Missionary Training Center. Alyssa performed ordinances as a temple worker and ultimately married in the temple.

As a Mormon, Alyssa checked every box. She *really* believed, and her dedication to the church is part of what makes this book so powerful. She intimately understands what it is like to be in your shoes.

As I read through each chapter, I was struck by how thoroughly Alyssa addresses the hurdles faced by those who leave the church. Her encouraging voice will support you with each step along this unknown path. Her compassionate and informed writing approaches the sensitive subject of faith deconstruction with a style that is personal, thoughtful, direct, and fearless. Her writing, influenced by her status as a millennial, is both accessible and relatable to audiences old and young.

In this book, you will find a comprehensive discussion of topics relevant to a recently disaffected Mormon, including "coming out" to family and friends, improving body image, healthy sexuality, discerning a new value set, mental health tips, and mindful substance exploration. Most of all, *How to Leave the Mormon Church* provides the reassurance that everything will (most likely) be okay. After a period of grieving, life can often become *healthier and more joyful* than it was as a believing Mormon.

One of the most painful realities I have witnessed over the past 20 years has been to see some Exmormons make hasty, emotional, and somewhat predictable decisions that have unnecessarily added *additional* suffering to the extant pain caused by their loss of faith. At times, these "rookie" Exmormon mistakes can lead to irreparable harm to individual health and well-being, as well as to treasured friendships and family relationships.

This book will help save you from many of these mistakes.

Each section is introduced with vignettes from Alyssa's life. These stories are poignant, humorous, and insightful. Helpful "Reflect and Write" exercises will help make the content applicable to your life. I echo Alyssa's suggestion in the book to journal regularly as you undergo this transformative time. A faith crisis is a massive loss, but in this book, Alyssa underscores this experience as a tremendous opportunity to learn about yourself and to connect more deeply with the world around you. *How to Leave the Mormon Church* uniquely celebrates the freedom and beauty of losing the church and finding yourself in the process.

In the last twenty years, there has been a massive wave of disaffection from Mormonism (and from organized religion in general) of almost epidemic proportions. Access to information and history is more straightforward than ever before. Yet, it is stunning that, at the time of my writing—January 2024—I cannot name a book that provides a "how to" for leaving the Mormon church that I am comfortable recommending. For twenty years, I have desperately wanted to write this book.

Well, Alyssa just wrote it. But better—because this book provides additional perspectives that I just can't.

May your painful and complicated journey out of Mormonism, or your own religious tradition, blossom into a beautiful gift of healing, self-discovery, positive growth, and improved relationships. This is my secular prayer.

Sincerely,
John Dehlin, Ph.D.
www.mormonstories.org

INTRODUCTION

I am the master of my fate,
I am the captain of my soul.

—*Invictus* by William Ernest Henley

I was Mormon before I was born. I'm not talking about the pre-earth life. I'm talking about the religious, temple-attending DNA passed to me from my polygamist ancestors who crossed the continent with Brigham Young. My ancestors followed Joseph Smith and fervently prayed for the salvation of their children—and their children's children.

My Mormon ancestry traces through polygamy and polyandry. My grandmother's grandmother remained a member through the rise of feminism and women's rights. My ancestors stayed in the church despite racist policies and sexist doctrine. My parents were married in the Albuquerque temple after my dad faithfully served his two-year mission in Minneapolis. In my family, it is baptism and saving ordinances all the way down.

After more than a century of faith in a tiny, American-born religion—there's me. And for the first few decades of my life, I completely fulfilled the dreams of my Mormon predecessors. My LDS resume was exemplary. My efforts and achievements weren't out of a misguided attempt to please parents or to show off to other members. The exceptional Mormon life I lived was out of the most sincere and genuine love for what I understood to be the gospel of Jesus Christ.

Baptized at eight, BYU at eighteen. As a child, I bore my testimony in my small Helena, Montana ward every single fast Sunday in that sing-songy voice we've all heard: "I'd like to bear my testimony: I know this church is true." Beehive president, Mia Maid president, Laurel President. Never watched an R-rated movie or drank caffeine. Later on my mission to Denver, Colorado, I became a Sister Training Leader after a few short transfers. After my mission, I was a temple worker, and I taught at the MTC.

At twenty-four, I married my husband, Jackson, in the Payson, Utah Temple. It was the day I prepared for my entire life. The day I dreamed of for years of Young Women's lessons about chastity, finding a righteous priesthood holder, and learning about my divine purpose as a woman. I read my patriarchal blessing over and over again, carefully highlighting sections about motherhood, marriage, and my future husband. As I whispered my new name, Adah, into Jackson's ear, I felt I had finally fulfilled my purpose.

This is not to say that, through all those years, there weren't countless moments that I paused and wondered—*wait, what?* In my Frankfort ward, the boys played basketball while the girls learned to cook. Driving home after my wedding reception, I flipped through cards from family and friends. Many were addressed to "Mr. and Mrs. Jackson Carpenter." My identity was erased over the course of the day. I've sat through "licked cupcake" chastity lessons. I recall getting into a heated argument with a young Elder in the MTC about whether or not polygamy was actually "over" or not. I said it was, while he said he was looking forward to its return.

A year after my wedding, I left the Mormon church. You're probably considering the same step if you're reading this book. Maybe you've already stepped off the Zion-bound wagon. The life built around the church's absolute truth evaporates.

Not everyone who leaves the church was raised in an orthodox Mormon family. Maybe you were a convert who spent a year or two in the church. Maybe your family was "less active," and as an adult, you "fell away."

No matter your affiliation with the Mormon church, it leaves a mark on your mind. The gospel, the culture, and the history of the church are almost impossible to disentangle from your identity. Leaving the Mormon church is more than taking your name off the church's records. When I had my first sip of wine, I thought, *There, I did it! I'm not Mormon anymore!* My glee was short-lived, and my path to leaving the Mormon church has been much longer and more complex than I ever anticipated.

Sometimes, I think of the many generations of Mormons before me. My forebears crossed the brutal landscape of the American West to follow a man they believed was a prophet of God. My many-greats grandparents gave up everything for the gospel. What might they think if they could see me now? I drink, my nose is pierced, I show my shoulders, I have several tattoos, and "fuck" is my most commonly used exclamation. At this point, only my blonde hair connects me back to my Mormon heritage.

And though I worry I am letting generations of ancestors down, I remember who they were at their core. I don't believe their essence was truly Mormon. Instead, they were driven to defy reason, safety, and comfort by a single trait: conviction. No one can doubt their faith. Belief was paired with immediate and significant action.

I will not break the time-tested tradition of conviction. When I left the church, I turned my back on my immediate and extended family. I abandoned decades of Mormon church membership. I disavowed my cultural community, ward, and entire belief system. When my early ancestors converted to Mormonism, they did the same.

I like to think the same wild conviction that drove my ancestors to convert to Mormonism and then risk death by crossing to Utah is the same wild conviction that drove me to leave the church. The same recklessness compelled me to write a book that may mean certain family members will never speak to me again.

Going against the grain is in my DNA. Fervor and zeal kept my family in the church for over one hundred years, and now the same proclivities flow through my veins. Perhaps I'm not so unlike my ancestors after all. I hope if they could see me, they would still be proud. The same goes for you, too.

The purpose of this book is not to convince you to leave the church, despite what the spicy title may suggest. This book is not *why* to leave the church. These chapters are for those who have already started the long trek out and need a companion for the journey. I am not a religious zealot as much as I am a recovering addict. I am not here to persuade you but to be a comforting voice. I know how hard it is to leave. I know how lonely it feels.

Mormonism dictates and moralizes every single aspect of your life. There is a "right way" to be married, have kids, spend money, have sex, interact with family, speak, talk, and dress. In discussing leaving with many friends and acquaintances, I'm always struck by the church's profound hold on one's consciousness. As a Mormon, you're not even alone in your mind—God can see and judge every thought.

In a popular movie called *The Truman Show*, the protagonist is born and raised inside a massive TV set. Every person he knows, from his mother and father to the neighbors across the street, are actors. He is the only person who is unaware his entire life is contrived. A director has carefully orchestrated every moment since his birth. There are spoilers in the following paragraphs.

In the film, he slowly but surely realizes the truth: reality is not what it seems. By the movie's end, he chooses to exit the set and enter the real world. After learning the truth of his manufactured reality, he decides to leave the only reality he's ever known. He walks through a dark door and onto a new life of his choosing.

This final scene was the inspiration for the cover of the book. I recommend watching the movie, even though you now know the ending. The character's experience can feel uncannily similar to the experience of leaving the church. In a few weeks or even in a single moment, the world is a fundamentally different place. I hope this book helps you take purpose-filled steps out of the Mormon church. May you find a brilliant new world waiting on the other side of the door.

My goal is to provide a resource to people who have already decided it's time to walk off the set of their Mormon lives: out the door of belief and into a new reality. Leaning on someone who understands the struggle can make all the difference. You are holding the book I wish I had when I left the church.

I wrote this book to give my fellow searchers and leavers something to reference throughout a years-long process of rethinking and rebuilding a life outside of Mormonism. I stopped wearing garments one year after I initially began questioning the gospel. It took about two years after leaving the church to decide how I felt about weed and three years before I could smoke it without a shred of guilt.

Each time I think I've conquered Mormonism, I realize there's some piece I haven't dealt with yet. I recognize a new aspect of my life that I continue to navigate like I did as a Mormon. Just when I think I've figured myself out, the church still has a hold on my mind in a way I have yet to confront and investigate.

I wrote this book for you, fellow traveler. It's what I wish I had as I walked away from a dogma I committed my entire existence to unblinkingly. This time in your life can feel out of control. It's exciting and horrifying and exhilarating and profoundly sad all at once. Take a deep breath and look around you. The sky is still a beautiful hue, the sun will still shine on your face, and you'll still have to pay taxes this year. It is going to be okay. It's going to be more than okay—it will be brilliant.

PRACTICAL CONSIDERATIONS

This book is split into two parts. Part One is dedicated to the initial faith crisis and aftermath, like sharing the news with your family and how to decide what to do after you've lost faith. Part Two explores aspects of life discouraged by Mormon culture and doctrine. You'll read about trying coffee for the first time, working through political opinions, and dealing with the buildup of Mormon shame swirling around your mind. I suggest beginning in Part One if you recently experienced a faith crisis. You may find more value in Part Two if you've been out of the church for a while.

Anyone considering leaving the church, in the process of leaving the church, or who has left the church will benefit from this book. My goal is to help provide a guide for the process of deconstructing religion. Religious deconstruction is the process of analyzing and pulling apart traditional religious beliefs. By pulling apart Mormon beliefs and examining the underlying foundation of our identity, we can begin to sculpt a new self. This process is not only about losing faith; it's also about finding a new path to walk.

The contents are most likely to be helpful to those who are within the first one to two years of leaving the church. However, I've spoken to many Exmormons who left the church years ago and are still too intimidated to try coffee. If you left the church at any point in your past and still find it rattling around in your brain, this book is for you.

Treat this book as a reference manual more than a novel. You can read it from cover to cover—one chapter after the other. However, jumping around and finding the most relevant information at any given time may be more helpful. Leaving the Mormon church is not a linear experience, so you may find yourself ready to learn about dating outside the church before telling your family you are entirely out.

There are also sections where you should pause to reflect and write. There are lined pages at the back of the book for this purpose. You can also keep a separate journal alongside this book to record your reactions and musings. Journaling is a vital part of processing your religious deconstruction. Most Mormons are so primed for journal writing the practice may as well continue. If you choose not to journal, write in the margins or read with a friend. Reading will be most powerful when paired with your own separate internalization.

This book covers the topics of depression, suicide, and self-harm. It also includes information about drugs, sex, and sexuality. The descriptions are very brief. If any or all of these topics are triggering or uncomfortable to read about, proceed with caution.

Throughout the book, I refer to anyone who has left the church as an "Exmormon." People use many different terms to define themselves after leaving the church. These terms include Post-Mormon, Ex-LDS, Former Mormon, and Non-Practicing Mormon. Each term is meant to capture a different version of what it means to leave the church.

I choose to use "Exmormon" exclusively to encapsulate all identities under a single term. Exmormon is the most commonly used term in groups online and in literature. My reliance on the term in this book is not to exclude identities but to speak to anyone who was once a member and is no longer Mormon.

The stories and experiences are shared as remembered and affirmed by me, the storyteller. Though I've recounted them as accurately as possible, the dialogue and descriptions are solely from my memory. The brain is a foggy, faulty machine, so please forgive any inaccuracies. Also of note, most of the names are changed to protect privacy.

Finally, do not feel you must do and experience everything in this book to become an Exmormon. There is no "right way" to be an Exmormon. You never have to try alcohol, get a tattoo, or have sex outside marriage to leave the church. I cover all these ideas and more in the book. However, the goal is to suggest exploration and openness, not to dictate a new prescribed path.

If you encounter an idea or sentiment that does not resonate, simply move on. You may return to the viewpoint in several months or years and feel ready to engage with it, or it may never be relevant. There is no value judgment here, merely suggestions and ideas. Don't let anyone tell you how to feel or who to be—that was the modus operandi of Mormonism. It is not mine.

ONE

FAITH CRISIS

Everything Comes Crashing Down

Live a good life. If there are gods and they are just, then they will not care how devout you have been, but will welcome you based on the virtues you have lived by. If there are gods, but unjust, then you should not want to worship them. If there are no gods, then you will be gone, but will have lived a noble life that will live on in the memories of your loved ones.

—Marcus Aurelius

In synchrony, velvet green aprons slid out of discreet silk kits. A wrinkled hand fell confidently into mine, the thumb pressing down on my knuckles. Spandex underwear hugged my thighs and breasts in odd places, and my index finger absently traced a thin knit line above my knee. My eyes briefly darted toward my dad, who was wearing a cloud-shaped hat. His face was impassable; no emotion moved across his brow—no evidence to suggest this ritual was peculiar or abnormal.

My brain desperately pleaded with my heart to love every passing moment of my first endowment. Trepidation was a sign of faithlessness. What did it reveal about me and my testimony if my initial reaction to the ceremony was pure disgust?

As panic and repulsion rattled through my anatomy, my smile widened, and I approached the veil with an unknown woman. Three knocks on a pole with a tiny, plastic mallet. A brief pause, and an older man's voice whispered from the other side of the curtain, "What is wanted?"

For a moment, my heart halted. How was I supposed to respond to this existential question from a disembodied voice? I had no idea what I wanted except to leave immediately. I glanced at the woman beside me, who began to speak, "Eve, having been true and faithful in all things, desires further light and knowledge by conversing with the Lord through the veil."

Another furrowed hand appeared at waist level, the fingers slightly spread in preparation. The woman smiled sedately and gestured toward the hand, nodding once. Her vacant expression was one you might see someone wearing at the grocery store like a clerk asked if she needed a receipt.

I held my breath and grasped the hand before me, fingers fumbling as the wrinkled hand jerked to slither into a precise position. The anonymous woman leaned in to whisper the correct words. Moisture began to condense on the tiny hairs of my ear as she methodically murmured three or four words at a time.

"Strength in the loins," she breathed into my ear.

"Strength in the loins," I parroted to the man through the veil.

Several minutes of this back and forth passed: the old man holding my hand and a woman pressed up next to me, quietly commanding me. Finally, the voice decreed, "Let her enter."

The hand pulled me through the gossamer curtain into a white room filled with light. Before I could process the new space, my mom settled before me. Her teeth gleamed with a smile, but

I could see threads of worry trailing across her eyes. I grinned back, attempting to crush the uneasiness inside me.

"How was it?" she asked.

"Wow. It was..." my voice hesitated, oscillating between brutal honesty and a white lie.

"It was really amazing." I finished, my smile widening.

"Good!" she sighed in relief.

Worry slipped away from her eyes. We sat in silence, looking around the ornate room. The conversation was over.

I felt hollowed out; every piece of the church felt tainted by the last few hours. Years of attending sacrament meetings, reading scriptures, and youth activities felt alien now. An angry feeling of betrayal simmered inside me. The apron, the veil, the handshakes, the new name—this was not the Mormon church of my childhood. After singing "I Love to See the Temple" for twenty-plus years, I finally knew what happened within the stone walls.

Later, alone in my bathroom, I took my new garments from the deflated plastic bag and set them on the counter. I didn't want them on my body. All I could see were the white bonnets and the green aprons around me at the temple. The *clunk, clunk, clunk* of the knocker against the metal pole still reverberated through my mind.

There was no peace or feeling of serenity, only a pit deep in my stomach. Somehow, the most sacred place on earth had made me feel like complete shit.

How was that possible?

After a few minutes of staring at the new garments, I took a deep breath. *Satan is trying to stop me from believing in the Church*, I weakly promised myself. *I know the Church is true. I believe in the gospel. That is enough for me.* I continued rationalizing while pulling the white nylon garments up my legs. The symbols sewn into the garment hovered over my knee, belly button, and chest.

Looking at myself in the mirror, my eyes filled with tears. I was wearing a costume—donning the disguise of belief. As I hid my repulsion in the temple, I concealed my body in the bathroom. My physical being no longer belonged to me but to the ceremony. Beneath the nondescript nylon was my living, breathing, conflicted self. From now on, I wouldn't only carry myself through the world; I would assume the heaviness of the temple, too.

Time passed, and the temple began to feel more normal. Soon, it was boring and repetitive. In the faithful years following, I struggled to shake the memory of how I felt during my first endowment. I put it on a shelf in the back of my mind. Whenever I accidentally picked up the thought again, I hastily put it back, shoving it far to the back to collect cobwebs. Wearing the garment as instructed, my torso became foreign to me. My mind twisted and turned as adeptly as possible to accept my body's new reality.

On my mission, missionaries swapped stories about the first time they went through the temple. It was usually a religious brag fest, and those who seemed the most "spiritual" had the most gleaming memories.

"I started crying when I walked into the celestial room. It felt like I was finally home."

"Everything about the temple was so inspired. My heart was so full of love for the Savior."

"It was such a special experience for me. I knew I was in God's house."

There was rarely an acknowledgment of how strange the temple is. There was no sign to indicate very few young people know anything about what happens during the endowment until they experience it firsthand. At times, I felt like the only broken one. Everyone else was profoundly inspired by the temple. If I was not, it meant I didn't love God enough.

Throughout my time in the church, I shoved doubt and worries deep, deep down—as far away as possible. And while I continued in the church for years after my first temple ordinance, by the time my shelf broke, there were hundreds of experiences crowding my shelf.

As a member, I consistently ignored any feeling the church could be false. I embraced unquestioning faith. Throughout my childhood and early adulthood, I wanted to be a good Mormon, not to be true to myself. I wanted perfect faith, but this was at the cost of pushing away any hesitancies or concerns. Looking back, I realize I was questioning my whole life.

While the temple stands out as a moment of massive crisis, my life was filled with shelf-crowding events. As you go through your faith crisis, you will likely reflect on these moments in your life. Someone set on belief will consistently disregard any indication their current life trajectory could be wrong. On the following pages are three examples of mindsets and moments that made me question my faith over the years. As you read, think of the moments you've placed on your own shelf.

• • •

Growing up, it was persistently clear that men were more important than women in the church. Sure, women were verbally shoved up onto a pedestal. I constantly heard remarks like, "Women are more spiritual," "Women don't need the priesthood because they already have the power of childbirth," "Being a mother is more important than having a career," and "Men may be the head, but women are the neck. Always remember, the neck turns the head."

Despite all the lip service, very little about the church resembled this reality. I wasn't exactly reading a lot of female names in the Bible and The Book of Mormon. When a woman miraculously appeared in lore, it was because she was either birthing babies or being a "help meet." The bishop and other men often visited us in Young Women's, but women never visited the Young Men's class to impart wisdom.

Sitting in a pew and looking up at who was on the pulpit (a literal pedestal), it was abundantly clear men were the most important. Typically, the people who hold power in this world do not need to be reminded they are special. There are a lot of days celebrating teachers and nurses, and none celebrating CEOs and investment bankers. No one needs to pat them on the head.

The treatment of women in the church quietly radicalized me to become more and more of a feminist over time, though I didn't quite realize it. As a Beehive President, Mia Maid President, and Laurel President, I felt great pride. On my mission, I was ecstatic to be called as a Sister Training Leader.

When I went through the temple, they still showed a video. There was a moment when Eve looked at Adam to covenant with him rather than God. When I first saw this portion of the movie, I was livid. The Mormon role of women was wholly summed up in one subtle turn of the torso and head. Even as she stands before God the Father, Eve still must turn away to make a promise to a man. Her movement was so purposeful and so illustrative. Men speak with God. Women quietly follow their husbands.

• • •

I recall learning the theory of evolution in my AP Biology class. Though teachers had touched on it before, it was my first time spending weeks learning about natural selection, alleles, and how to complete a Punnett square. Evolution fascinated me, and I checked out a tattered copy of *The Origin of Species* to read in bed at night. Though I was aware that evolution contradicted a creationist narrative, I naively felt they could exist in tandem.

At a Wednesday youth activity, I made a joke about the survival of the fittest during a basketball game. A bishopric member overheard me and asked me to step into the hall. His face transformed into a red grimace. I remember shrinking down as he said, "There is no such thing as evolution. It is very disrespectful for you to bring that idea into a church building."

He paused, and I whispered an apology while staring at the floor. In a condescending tone, he murmured, "We did not come from monkeys," as he walked back into the carpeted gym. The next day, I returned the book by Darwin and stopped drawing double helix structures on the margins of my class notes. I wanted to be a good Mormon, and in a battle between science and God, science would get tossed to the curb every time.

• • •

In 2015, the church unveiled a new policy restricting the children of gay parents from being baptized. I lay in bed reading articles and comments on Facebook and Reddit. The second article of faith ran through my mind, "We believe that men will be punished for their own sins, and not for Adam's transgression."

I was already unsure if homosexuality was really a sin, and restricting baptism from a child was somehow a new level of cruelty. The kids were being punished for their parent's "sins," not their own. The policy was out of line with my doctrinal understanding of personal accountability, agency, and the supreme importance of baptism for all who desire to receive it.

There was no policy restricting the children of murderers, rapists, or felons from being taught by the missionaries and baptized. Somehow, being gay was worse than any other possible choice.

I lay awake past midnight, staring at the ceiling. The familiar, angry knot in my abdomen tightened, as it had in the temple and many times before. *Maybe it's not true*, I allowed myself to whisper in the quiet of my mind.

• • •

My three examples of questioning Mormon teachings and culture do not mean I never loved the church. I can also share hundreds of positive experiences. Girls camp, testimony meetings, lessons on my mission, blessings, and Family Home Evenings were moments of pure Mormon joy.

I chose to serve a mission. I decided to attend BYU. I got married in the temple. All this despite my frustrations with how women were treated in the church. I carried the faith even though I felt the 2015 church policy was unfair and against my doctrinal understanding of agency. Whenever I felt discord between the church and my humanity, my mind quickly shifted focus back to how much happiness I found in Mormonism.

I continued to attend the Mormon church despite my experience in the temple. I served a mission even though I felt the church treated women as second-class citizens. My heart chose God even though my brain understood science. It was entirely apparent gay people deserved to love whoever they chose—but I still spouted doctrinal homophobia for years into my adult life.

So many touchpoints indicated the church was not what I thought it was. You may also be unsuccessfully attempting to doubt your doubts before you doubt your faith. Even considering the church may be untrue is acutely scary and painful. You may want to run away from any evidence hinting it could be false.

On my last day in an LDS church, I walked out in the middle of a Relief Society meeting and drove home. The same night, I drove into the snowy mountains and parked in an empty lot. I bowed my head and began to cry and pray all at once. "Please, please Heavenly Father," I begged, "Are you still there? Please, I cannot do this without you."

As much as I no longer believed in Joseph Smith or The Book of Mormon, I desperately needed God and Jesus to exist. I wanted this so badly that it was a real, physical pain.

Letting go of Mormonism was harrowing, but letting go of God was unfathomable. In the next few weeks, I frantically fought to retain some sort of belief. On the road out of Mormonism, it seems everyone walks this same path. There's a desire to continue with religion and belief on your terms. Maybe you don't want to wear garments anymore, but you want to continue praying to a loving Father.

As the world comes unwound, the mind attempts to protect itself. This may mean you continue in the church even after learning details about Joseph Smith and his many wives. You may keep your peace by believing in God after losing your testimony in priesthood power. Humans search for a connection back to emotional safety if the world unravels at the seams.

These mental gymnastics are called cognitive dissonance. All humans, religious or irreligious, engage in cognitive dissonance. It occurs when there is a clash between what someone thinks, believes, or values and their actual behavior. In response, individuals may attempt to rationalize, justify, or modify their behavior to reduce this cognitive dissonance.

Someone who values fair worker treatment likely still wears clothing produced in Chinese sweatshops. While most people want workers to be treated well, consumers value saving their money even more. Most people who believe climate change is real and a worldwide threat still drive a gas-guzzling car each day. Day-to-day convenience is a higher value than long-term environmental wellness on a global scale.

Cognitive dissonance may push someone who consumes fast fashion to occasionally shop at thrift shops. You may save money to buy an electric car or switch your electric provider over to renewable energy to close the dissonance gap. As a young woman, I set up and took down folding chairs, even though it was a task designated for the young men. This was my feeble attempt to resolve the inconsistency between how I perceived myself and who my religion told me I was.

For many people, the shelf where you place your doubts grows increasingly cluttered over the years with various experiences and unsettling information. When someone's shelf breaks, it's because the cognitive dissonance load becomes too heavy to maintain.

A faithful temple-attending member finds their testimony broken into one million pieces overnight. On closer examination, many tiny experiences or moments throughout time culminated in a final, grand crescendo. For Exmormons, the mind's defenses crumble after a lifetime of rationalizing and justifying membership in the church.

My shelf was too heavy for me. I couldn't shove away the accumulated experience and truth any longer. Your testimony is no longer sufficient to hold back all the reasons why the church feels and is wrong. You can only live with cognitive dissonance for so long.

REFLECT AND WRITE

To begin this process of reassembly, you have to take the time and space to be. Do not allow the pain and anguish you're experiencing to rob you of what you can learn about yourself and who you are.

Find a quiet place to write answers to the following questions. Write in the back of this book or a separate notebook. Answer one question or all of them, or simply free-write whatever comes to mind. Don't worry about getting it right; focus on what comes to mind and write it down.

- What do you fear most about leaving the church?
- What do you look forward to?
- What values do you consider most important in life?
- What personal values would you maintain if you transition out of the church?

COMFORTABLE WITH DISCOMFORT

If your shelf is broken on the ground, you are likely wondering, "Now what?" After struggling with a faith crisis, it's incredibly difficult to know what to do next. You may feel paralyzed with indecision and unsure how to move forward.

When I was in the process of losing my faith, there were many tears and late nights. And whether you're sure the church is not for you, or if you're questioning, please pause and know everything will be okay. You may not feel it now, but I promise life outside the church is big and beautiful.

Losing the comfort of the church is scary. The road to deconstructing a high-demand religion is long and winding. Mormonism likely feels like the fabric of your being. The church may currently feel inexorably linked with who you are.

As your faith crisis develops, you will likely experience an almost day-to-day change in your beliefs. Questions about telling your family the news and trying a cup of coffee may swirl through your mind. As you take one day and one moment at a time, be patient with change. Try to enjoy learning about yourself and your new beliefs. Get comfortable with the new journey you now find yourself taking.

To wean a child from a comfort blanket, you can cut it into smaller pieces, ultimately leaving one small corner for them to keep in their pocket. Even one tiny square of a beloved object is still comforting. After a period of time, the parent may covertly remove the square from the child's possession entirely. The weaning process is complete.

As a Mormon, my security blanket was massive—I had prayer, an eternal family, scripture study, and countless other ways to seek support when I went through a difficult time. After I initially left, the blanket was cut smaller and smaller. I no longer believed in temple covenants. The Book of Mormon became meaningless. But I held tightly to my one remaining square—the hope that maybe, just maybe, God might still exist.

Two years after leaving the church, I woke up to realize I wasn't even agnostic anymore. The last little ragged square of my security blanket was nowhere to be found. I struggled to cope with the final death of belief. In a moment of panic or stress, I would still reflexively pray. My emotional fingers twitched, habitually searching for the soft comfort of my little square of blanket.

The Alyssa of then and the Alyssa of now may look and act the same, but we are fundamentally different people. She really, really wanted God to be real. The Alyssa writing this book laughs at the most irreligious jokes. The Alyssa writing this book never prays. The You here and now is not the same You who reads chapter six or ten of this book. And in ten years, you'll reflect on each version of yourself. You may see a similar image: a frightened child clinging to their tattered old blanket, not ready to face the scary world without it.

Certainty is a human urge. We want to know exactly what to believe and to maintain that belief and identity throughout a whole lifetime. Admitting we were wrong in the past is hard. It is even harder to admit we may be wrong currently, in the here and now.

Though we desire internal consistency, the passage of time may fundamentally influence who we are and our outlook. Allow space to carry beliefs if they positively impact your life and existence. But know that you may change in the future, and it is better to accept uncertainty than to cling to absolutism.

There is no rush to get anywhere. Your feelings and beliefs will likely morph for the next several years and your lifetime. This frustrates most people. Mormon doctrine teaches beliefs are not meant to transform. You may be prompted to grow in faith, but you should never radically change your belief system.

You are likely absorbing massive amounts of information from many different, conflicting sources. The initial phase of losing your testimony is a tornado of indecision and confusion.

On any given day, you wake up to a text from your dad asking if you're still praying. Opening your scriptures, you search the old verses that used to bring you so much comfort, but it's hard to focus. While you read, you remember something about the history of The Book of Mormon you read online. You open your phone to see if you can find the article again.

As you scroll through Google, you open a related search result. The article aims to destroy the historicity of The Book of Mormon. You text the link to your sibling to get an opinion from someone who is simultaneously faithful and nonjudgmental. You're still trying to keep your questioning private.

A few hours later, you get a call from a previous youth leader in your home ward. Your mom told them you're struggling. They're calling to try to help you. Or are they trying to *save* you? The motive is murky, and you politely end the call without saying much.

That night, you kneel to pray like you have thousands of times before. You do your best to feel inspired and fulfilled, but once you're on your knees, it feels forced. After a few minutes of feeling awkward and unnatural, you give up.

If you're like me in those early days, you are a wrecking ball swinging wildly through space. One moment, you're quietly gliding through the air. In the next, your testimony is smashed to pieces. Within hours, you can feel a supreme sense of faith and belief and then sink into a trench of skepticism and doubt.

There is no safe harbor in these early days, weeks, and months. When I went through what you now face, my heart could turn on a dime. After speaking with my bishop, I would leave feeling triumphant. *My faith crisis is finally behind me*, I would promise myself. Later, unable to fall asleep, I would get sucked into reading an analysis of the Joseph Smith Papyri. I would feel as lost as ever.

You may feel as if you are being stretched and pulled in two. It is impossible to forget or discount the times you stood before a congregation of people and proclaimed, "I know this church is true."

On my mission, I uttered this phrase over and over and over again. I stopped shoppers in Target aisles and chased down people walking to get their mail. I can barely read my mission journal because each entry is the same reworded testimony over and over again for five hundred and forty-seven days' worth of entries. I was absolutely positive the church was God's truth on earth.

Now, I hardly recognize that missionary. I can hardly believe that in this same single life, I performed washing and anointing ordinances as a temple worker and passed out drunk in an Airbnb after playing flip-cup. These two disparate people could not believably occupy the same consciousness. And yet—here I am.

You may feel you'll never be able to move past the Mormon You. Maybe you want to believe and disbelieve all at once. Honor all the people sitting at the table inside your head. Each identity and each version of yourself exists there for a reason. Instead of shaming any one of them, listen to what they have to say.

REFLECT AND WRITE

- Write about your experiences with church history and teachings throughout your life. When you learned something controversial or disappointing, how did you feel? How do you feel about what you learned now?
- Is there a time when your identity or values were at odds with church teachings? How did people around you react?
- Write a personal experience you had in the church that impacted you. Why does it matter now?
- What are things you are still sure of? What are things you still need to figure out?

THE UPSIDE OF NOTHING

In the chaotic world of being human, there will be no grand endpoint of certainty. Life is a mish-mash of searching for meaning, value, happiness, and truth. The time of stating, "I know..." has passed. This is the era of "I'm not sure" and "I'm still figuring things out."

Look forward to the future: your life is a blank canvas. You have the freedom to choose the meaning and purpose of your existence. Life is an opportunity to exist on your terms, unbound by religious, familial, or cultural expectations. When my shelf first hit the ground, these ideas terrified me. I only wanted my security blanket. Now, the concept of making my own meaning is exhilarating.

I left the Mormon church seven years ago. At this juncture, I do not believe in any kind of God. I am an optimistic nihilist. This is a philosophical belief that life has no inherent meaning or purpose. While on its surface, this may sound discouraging and devoid of joy, I find the meaninglessness of life and the insignificance of human existence empowering.

If nothing matters, then nothing really matters! Life is about joy and finding purpose in the present. There is no eternity to prepare for, only the moments that pass before us right now. Ironically, The Book of Mormon accurately depicts this philosophy in 2 Nephi 28:7: "Eat, drink, and be merry, for tomorrow we die."

This book will be tinged with my own optimistic nihilism, though that doesn't mean you'll land where I have. My claim to Exmormon authority is that I've done this myself. One friend recently referred to me as her "Exmormon guru," which may be my proudest title received to date. After baptism, a mission, and a temple marriage, I left the Mormon church. And I've lived happily and abundantly since exiting. No person or entity tells me how to live; I choose my journey.

This is the best part of losing your faith: the realization that after a lifetime of seeking direction for your life from scriptures, church leaders, and God, you finally have permission to get guidance *from yourself.* Imagine that. You authorize yourself to be the first and last say on your existence. The time of appealing to some external moral authority is over. *You are the god of your world.*

Here, in Chapter One, you may not be ready for optimistic nihilism. And you may not be ready for the not-so-subtle endowment reference. However, you are probably prepared to hear the good news that life can be wonderful outside the church. There are R-rated movies to watch and lattes to drink. Sunday afternoons are left wide open. There's ten percent back in your bank account, and there are cocktails to clink together and say, "Cheers!" with the ones you love.

Better yet, there is the freedom to finally look inward and ask yourself, "Who am I?" and "What do I want from life on this little blue marble?" The upside of nothing—of no God and no church—is EVERYTHING. Rules and constraints and judgment and doctrines and policies have vanished. Your world is teeming with endless possibilities.

GOOD IN THE PAST, BETTER IN THE FUTURE

Even as you peek toward a future outside the church, you may also reflect on the good that Mormonism brought into your life. You may be concerned about how you'll make friends outside the church or raise a future family without good Mormon values. Finding a new community outside the church is daunting and may not even feel possible.

This is the duality of losing a religion like Mormonism. Living a life without the limitations of Mormonism sounds thrilling but also paralyzing. Many people benefit from being a church member, even if there are problematic doctrines and policies. The church provides an environment where many people feel they thrive. Connections rooted in Mormonism run deep.

Ultimately, the church is false. I left because The Book of Mormon is fabricated, and Joseph Smith was only a man, not a prophet, directed by a supreme being. Despite these realities, I still experienced significant goodness as a member. I didn't serve a mission because I never had a testimony or hated the church. I gave away all those days to Mormonism because I loved it.

My depression was pretty severe as a kid. After I turned fourteen, I began cutting and using self-harm as a coping mechanism. This is something I've done occasionally throughout my life, a product of depression and anxiety. These manifestations of my unhappiness continued into college, and now, even as a mom of two, sometimes I still fall back into old habits.

During my first year at BYU, my parents got divorced. Divorce is hard on anyone, but after eighteen years and countless lessons on forever families, it was devastating. I spent weeks holed up in my dorm room, only leaving for class and church.

Cutting became a crutch, and I went from using it monthly to weekly. Sometimes, I left class early to self-harm and feel the sweet numbness of nothingness. In the hours after, I always felt repulsed by myself and my actions. My mind began circling back to the concept of suicide, and each time, it was more difficult to push away. I was scared that something irreversible would happen if I didn't get help.

Eventually, I decided to confide in my bishop about the situation. Sitting in a chair across from him, I was embarrassed and ashamed. Over his head was a painting of Christ comforting a dark-haired woman who cried in his lap. I spoke with my bishop at length, and he encouraged me to see a therapist. He said I needed to see a professional. I explained I didn't want my parents to know what I was going through.

My mom knew about my cutting in high school, and I knew she would be upset if she found out I was doing it again. I didn't want to introduce the pain and disappointment of my choices into my parents' lives. When I saw a therapist, my dad's insurance would be billed, and they would figure out what was happening.

The bishop tried to reassure me: there was no way my parents would be upset that I was seeking help. I wouldn't budge—if it was on my dad's insurance, there was no way I would go.

After going back and forth on this, my bishop said something that changed my life. "If you won't go on your family's insurance, let me pay for it."

Shocked, I responded, "No, you can't do that for me. I don't have a car, anyways, so there's no way I can get to the appointments."

"My wife doesn't work. She can drive you every week."

Tears began falling from my eyes. I was some random freshman in a massive young adult ward at BYU. It was clear I was a worthless piece of broken garbage. "Okay," I took a deep breath, "I'll go."

That man paid for my therapy out of his own pocket for over a year. And every week, his wife picked me up from campus and drove me fifteen minutes each way to my weekly meeting. While I spoke with the therapist, the bishop's wife sat in her car and read a book. Those therapy sessions saved my heart and my life.

I do not hate the church. Arguably, the church is what ultimately saved my life, as it provided a way for me to come into contact with this immensely generous couple. The bishop and his wife provided a lifeline at one of the darkest moments of my existence. No negative experience in the church or awful church history will ever steal this sweet story from me.

As you sit in your chair reading this, I am sure you can easily remember happy moments from your membership in the church. Powerful and kind leaders. Close friendships with youth. Tearful prayers ending in peace. These moments of joy shine bright despite the history of polygamy or anti-gay rhetoric in conference talks. It's confusing, and it is why people stay in the church for their whole lives. Your brain pushes away the bad and focuses solely on happiness.

The church can be false while still creating a lot of good. The good can exist even though the church also perpetuates a tremendous amount of bad. You can love the church and the people in the church and still be justified in leaving it behind. You can leave the church and simultaneously love it.

I found such community and kindness in the church. So much of my fear was wrapped up in what I was leaving behind. There was nowhere else to go for the level of compassion I found in my bishop.

But since I've been out, I've discovered Mormons do not have a monopoly on human goodness. It turns out all types of people can be loving and giving and welcoming. Since leaving the church, I have constantly interacted with empathetic and altruistic people. I've made new friends and formed deep connections. Finding a new community after leaving the church has been challenging but not impossible.

I have found people who provide wisdom and support in difficult times. I've connected with Exmormons and with never Mormons. My new friend group doesn't shoot me side-eye if I watch R-Rated movies or say *FUCK* when I drop something on the ground. They don't mind when I wear tank tops or shorts that show my thighs. Since leaving the church, I've found abundant friendship with none of the judgment.

The world is full of good people. There were good times in the past as a member, but I promise it can get even better in the future. Being part of a religious community is great, but finding your own community of people who love you regardless of belief is even better.

BRAVE BUT FRAUGHT ENDEAVOR

Even after you've experienced your faith crisis, you may not be ready to leave it all in the past. Some people want to continue to attend on their own terms. Leaving your faith and community is a huge step, and some people who initially question their faith have tremendous hope for the church. This sprouts from the goodness they've experienced as a member.

When you love something, you don't simply leave it behind. After losing a testimony, some people aim to change the church from within rather than leave it behind entirely. This is valorous logic, and I think it works for some people some of the time.

You may speak up for any gay members of your ward and openly support LGBTQIA+ people. During Sunday School and in church talks, you may try to proactively talk about church history and discuss the facts of the early church.

Changing the church from within also might mean practicing the religion in a nontraditional way. When I went to BYU, I was shocked to realize my brand of Mormonism was not universal. Some people I met lived more strictly, like one friend who never wore makeup and only wore dresses that covered her wrists and skirts which fell to her calves. One roommate listened to pop music in her room on Sunday. I always clutched my pearls when I walked past her door.

One version of changing the church from within may look like living a less rules-obsessed version of the gospel. Despite the sinful music coming from my roommate's room, I am fairly certain she still loved Heavenly Father. At the time, I felt like I could barely be friends with her, but I also recognize I may still be in the church if I had been raised with that version of Mormonism. Those with the strictest Mormon childhoods seem to be some of the first to leave after becoming adults.

Church leadership has been steering the church toward mainstream doctrines and policies. Sunday service is two hours long instead of three. There's a new *For the Strength of Youth* pamphlet with significantly fewer hard-line rules. Women don't have to cover their faces during the endowment session anymore. Many of these changes seem to signal the church is legitimately changing from within.

If you aim to change the church from within, I commend you. Challenging the status quo of a large, traditional organization is onerous and requires grit and bravery. Once I stopped believing in the core gospel and the fundamental tenets of the religion, I couldn't attend anymore. Staying for the community and the gospel was not worth it to me. I was unwilling to continue paying ten percent of my income, wear garments, and hold a calling.

If you have lost your faith but aren't ready to let the church go, you can try to change it from within. Or maybe, in the same way I fervently hoped to still believe in God, you will persist on this path for a few days, weeks, or months and ultimately choose to leave for good.

There is no need to plan years in advance or contrive some grand plan to infiltrate the inner culture of the church. As the Bible sagely instructs, "Take therefore no thought for the morrow... sufficient unto the day is the evil thereof."

Keep membership in whatever capacity makes sense for you, but don't put yourself in emotional danger. Sometimes, we hold tight to the things we love, even if they hurt us. Reforming the church from within may be a noble cause, but it may also be a bit of religious Stockholm syndrome. The mantra of this book is to listen to your heart and be kind to yourself. Do what makes you happy and protect your mental health.

Be patient and take your time regardless of your approach or how long the process takes. Buy a new leather-bound journal for yourself to chronicle these moments of your life. Ask yourself, "Why am I doing this?" and "What are my motives?" and "What do I hope to accomplish by taking this course of action?"

EXAMINE EVERY PIECE

A crucial part of leaving the church is pausing often to reflect on your past experiences and current state of being. Write down memories of your past and, in turn, connect the memories with the thoughts and feelings of leaving. Learn about your mind. Reflect on who you were and what you will become after the dust settles.

One of my biggest regrets after leaving was how little I stopped to do this one thing. Once my testimony evaporated, I attempted to sprint through the process of religious deconstruction. This left me with a lot of unresolved confusion and angst. As you leave, allow yourself to do it slowly. Leaving a church so profoundly rooted in your soul cannot be done overnight.

You may physically stop attending church, but you cannot remove all the habits, messages, practices, conceptions, and cognitive biases from your soul for a long time. Like assembling a

10,000-piece puzzle, every piece must be inspected, considered, sorted, and carefully placed.

Growing up in the church means your identity has an entirely distinct Mormon dimension. You and Mormon You were so inexorably linked. It may be mind-bending for you to imagine a difference between the two—the You outside Mormon You. Dissecting that layer from yourself and figuring out what is You and what is Mormon You is a years-long process. Carefully explore your mind and decide what to keep and what to throw out. As you try to make sense of this chaos, step back and breathe.

REFLECT AND WRITE

- How are you feeling after reading the first chapter of this book? How are you feeling about deciding to buy and read this book?
- List three personal beliefs you're willing to reconsider or explore further.
- Think of a time you had an experience with the spirit (or what you thought was the spirit). How does that experience make you feel now?
- Describe one or two significant life events that made you want to leave the church. What happened? Why did it make you want to leave?

TWO
PRECIPICE
Let Go So You Can Fly

It is better to live your own destiny imperfectly than to live an imitation of someone else's life with perfection.

—Bhagavad Gita

When I was a senior in high school, my dad gave me a father's blessing. It foretold I would and should be a teacher as my life's calling. At Brigham Young University, I declared my major in the first week. No other possibilities entered my mind. I didn't talk to teachers to see what they had experienced. I was a soft-spoken introvert but didn't look inward to consider if I had the proper disposition. When my dad uttered those words, I knew I would be a teacher.

My dreams of becoming a writer disappeared overnight. Any other path—biology, painting, psychology, and photography—vanished from my mind like ice on summer pavement. This was a *revelation*, straight from God. Throughout my four-year degree,

I never wavered. I never considered anything else. Teaching was God's path for me, and my feet walked with purpose.

My first year of teaching ninth grade at American Fork Junior High was the stuff of nightmares. My windowless classroom was a rectangle of cinder blocks, and the teacher's lounge was an even smaller rectangle of cinder blocks. I never saw the sun on weekdays.

Students were remarkably rude to me. I looked too young. The secretary mistook me for a student on my first day in the building. A parent told me that her son didn't respect me because I reminded him of his older sister.

Students wrote mean notes and slid them under my door. Some notes were run-of-the-mill, *you're ugly*, or *everyone hates you. Other messages, like one on an anonymous feedback survey, got more specific: You are so stupid. I hate your handwriting. It looks like a child. I should be the teacher instead of you because you are fucking dumb.*

A group of boys would skip other classes and bang on my classroom door. Startled, I would jump and yelp. Students inside the class would film my reaction and post it on Snapchat. At one point, a student rolled a smoke bomb under my classroom door, and the school was evacuated because someone thought there was a real fire.

The leadership at the school said, "Kids will be kids." I never expected to be bullied as a teacher, but it seemed common. A friend who was teaching at a nearby school told me male students would secretly take photos of her butt during class. They would post the pictures to a shared Instagram account dedicated to her butt. The page had over 1,000 followers.

After the first month of school, the panic attacks started. My clock went off at 5:30 am, and the dread sunk deep into my stomach. Sometimes, I called in sick, hyperventilating on my side of the phone line. But I couldn't quit—this was my calling.

As shared in the last chapter, I had struggled with mental health issues my whole life, but this job was making it much worse. I recognize many people are teachers and go through similar experiences and are completely fine. Teaching is an arduous and often thankless occupation. Of course, I was aware of this fact throughout my year at the school. I wasn't proud that teaching impacted my mental health so significantly. At one point, even the school secretary suggested I see a therapist. I was ashamed I couldn't do this basic job so many people do, year after year, with no problems.

I attempted to ignore the panic attacks as much as possible. God was trying me. He was testing me and my faith. Any doubt I chose the wrong career was quickly dismissed and placed high on my shelf. Night after night, I would cling to Jackson, trying to dispel the awful sense of foreboding about going to work the next day.

Anyone familiar with mental health on any level knows this truth: ignoring the problem makes it worse. By January, I was cutting myself. In my first year of teaching, it got pretty bad. I would hide in the bathroom, trying to cope and treat the pain. Just as I had after my parent's divorce, I started thinking about ending my life.

On my mission, I often taught investigators that God gives us challenges because he loves us. God is our father, and a father allows his children to learn through difficult experiences. "When a toddler is learning to walk," I would cheerily share, "the parents let the child fall to the ground. Children fall hundreds of times before they learn to walk. God lets us fall because he wants us to learn to walk by ourselves—but he is with us the whole time."

While driving to and from work, I would consider this analogy. In those quiet moments, my anxiety was deafening. It didn't feel like God was letting me gently fall to the ground under his watchful care. Instead, he was grasping my head by the nape, forcing me underwater, refusing to let me up to breathe. This loving father of mine was driving me straight toward suicide.

Betrayed and confused, I couldn't make sense of it. Since receiving the blessing, I doggedly pursued my goal to become a teacher. My faith had not wavered; my obedience was wholehearted. Most people would look at my situation and would say I should've left the job. As a teaching intern, I made $19,000 that year. Certainly, I could've found an easier way to make money with my degree. I should've quit if the panic attacks and depression were so bad. But leaving meant disobeying God and turning my back on his commandment. Giving up was impossible.

Though I hated to admit how weak I felt, I knew one thing: persisting on this path would kill me. Striving to obey and follow God while casting myself aside would be ruinous. One Sunday night, I sat in the car alone, staring off over the interstate. I anxiously thought of going to work the following day. The blackness felt immense, like it would swallow me whole.

Looking out across the valley, I had a novel thought. *What if this isn't a test? Maybe God isn't punishing me or testing me—maybe God simply isn't real?* The thought reverberated through my body. *God isn't real.* My brain exploded a little. Pieces of my life in the church floated before me like the lights across the valley. I considered all the times I had felt this idea, then quickly hid the thought away like a dirty secret.

While I sat there, I remembered another time when powerful personal revelation was utterly incorrect. I was in college and preparing to serve a mission. One day, I was sitting in the temple, waiting for my turn to do baptisms for the dead.

Sitting in the pew, I had a profound, spiritual feeling about where I would serve my mission. In the holy walls of the house of the Lord, I believed God told me I would serve my mission in Italy. The thought slammed into me out of nowhere. I hadn't been praying to receive revelation on this topic; it simply came to me. Bursting into tears, I left the baptismal area early.

Once I was home in my BYU apartment, I wrote in my journal: *I received the most powerful revelation in the temple today. I am going to serve my mission in Italy. It was such an intense experience. I am as sure I will serve a mission in Italy as I am sure God exists.*

I can still read this entry in my journal. I even shared the news with a couple of people who were very close to me. A month or so later, my mission call arrived in the mail. I hiked to the top of Y Mountain to open it, viewing it as a mini religious pilgrimage. Between the tall pine trees, I sat on a rock and began carefully ripping the top seal. It was pomp and circumstance for nothing—I already knew where the mission call would direct me to serve the Lord.

A familiar-looking page fell out of the envelope. It was the same page I had seen many friends hold, shaking, as they read their mission call. I placed the envelope over the page to conceal the message and to keep my eyes from jumping ahead.

I read slowly, "Dear Sister Grenfell, You are hereby called to serve as a missionary for The Church of Jesus Christ of Latter-Day Saints. You are assigned to labor in the Colorado Denver North Mission."

Stopping abruptly, I read the line again. And then I read it again. Colorado Denver North Mission. My eyes glanced up and out across the trees, almost scanning for someone who could address the apparent mistake. Disoriented, I tucked the page back into the envelope and began stumbling down the mountain.

By the time I made it to the base, I convinced myself that the "revelation" I received in the temple was a mistake. I confused my hope to serve an international mission with a message from God. Obviously, my divine calling was to be fulfilled in the middle-class suburbs of Colorado. There it was, enshrined in print on paper. As I had time and time again, I shoved away this piece of proof.

God could not lie; I was the problem. When the day came, I reported to the MTC. I served a faithful mission. As much as I attempted to embrace my mission call to Denver, I spent the year and a half wondering, deep in the back of my mind, why I wasn't in Italy. The feeling in the temple had been so powerful it had brought me to tears. It was the same exact feeling I had used to legitimize the existence of God and the veracity of The Book of Mormon. If I was wrong about the mission call, how could I *know* I was right about the rest of it?

Years after that moment in the temple, I found myself in Utah again, sitting in my car. I finally allowed myself to fully consider the implications of my Italy revelation. The journal entry still clung to my mind. *I am as sure I will serve a mission in Italy as I am sure God exists.*

Now, it felt like if I reread the journal entry, it was a prophecy for the future. I didn't serve my mission in Italy, and God does not exist. Teaching was not my dream. It was a path I followed blindly after a blessing from my dad. These "revelations" were simply my own desires, along with the hopes and dreams of the people close to me. What I believed was "the spirit" was actually my neural pathways pushing me toward a desired path.

"God isn't real." I tried saying it out loud, in a whisper. The past washed away, and I thought of the future. How could I raise children without the church? How could I tell Jackson? What happened after death? How could I tell my mom, dad, and sisters? What was my life without God and the church? Who was I without the spirit to guide me?

When I got home, I warily told Jackson my fears. We spoke for a long time, and he was surprised but very understanding. Chapter Three includes a longer explanation of this conversation. "I love you no matter what you believe," he calmly said, hugging me while I cried.

After he fell asleep, I typed "Mormon church is not true" into Google and clicked on the first result. Soon, I found the CES Letter. I read for hours. I had ignored church history for years because I was so confident about my spiritual experiences with Mormonism. Spiritual revelation could not lead me to truth. Suddenly, history and facts were supremely important.

The next morning, I went through the motions of a typical workday. On the inside, it felt as if I was ripping into pieces. Like my arms and legs and fingers and toes and mind couldn't stay held together without a belief in the church. I had summited a mountain after years of slowly climbing. The night before, I had crested the peak, and now I was speeding toward the base faster than I had ever before. Momentum was mounting, but I had no idea what waited for me at the bottom.

FINAL ATTEMPT

My faith crisis played out over about three months. Three months of waffling back and forth on the ledge between "maybe I can still make this work" and "I don't believe any of this anymore." Those few months were torture. The constant reversing between believing and unbelieving was exhausting. Giving up the faith of my childhood and my life felt impossible; I told myself it was a phase. Maybe I could fake it. I angrily demanded of myself, "Just believe."

My mind buzzed with the same core thoughts in the months leading up to my exit from the church. Like a pop song set to replay, the lyrics hummed no matter where I was. Walking through the grocery store by our apartment, *God isn't real*, tap danced through my mind. Eating lunch with an old mission companion, *the church isn't true, nagged at my brain.* Sitting in sacrament meeting and listening to the talks, I thought, over and over again, *The Book of Mormon is false.*

One Sunday morning, I told Jackson I didn't want to go to church. Though he was feeling similarly about Mormonism, he still decided to attend. We had the same conversation the following Sunday, and he went to church while I stayed behind. While he was gone, I manically switched between scrolling through the Exmormon subreddit and staring at my scriptures.

A desperate piece of me remained, still hoping for some glorious, undeniable spiritual experience. Glimpses of life in the church would slip through my mind from time to time: watching my children dip beneath the water during their baptism or peacefully praying at night with my husband. I wasn't ready to let go of the life my ancestors dreamed up for me, at least not yet.

On the third Sunday, I decided to go again. Maybe it was still possible to recapture what I had lost. I sat on the blue fabric pew and listened during sacrament. I stared at my hands throughout the meeting, revulsion slipping through my veins. By going to church and participating in the service, I was endorsing a lie. When someone handed the sacrament to me, I briskly passed it on to Jackson. He passed it along as well. My eyes stayed glued to my hands.

During Relief Society, a woman explained there was no lesson prepared due to a calendar issue. She explained, "I felt impressed during sacrament that we should all take turns bearing our testimonies of Joseph Smith."

She set a photo of the Mormon prophet on the table before the lectern. He was framed in gold and placed on a lacy, white runner. After a pause, people started standing up and sharing.

One woman tearfully read lines from "Praise to the Man." Another read the quote, "Joseph Smith, the Prophet and Seer of the Lord, has done more, save Jesus only, for the salvation of men in this world, than any other man that ever lived."

The repulsion I felt during sacrament meeting stretched to cover my whole body, enveloping my fingers and toes and the tips of my hair. No one mentioned polygamy or polyandry. No one mentioned his treasure hunting or his misinterpretation of the

Egyptian papyri. Somehow, in all my years of testimony meetings, none of these well-documented facts about Joseph Smith ever surfaced.

Every person in the room was parroting the same flowery testimony about Joseph Smith. Each person reworded the same sentiments over and over again. The words "I know," "I feel," and "prophet of God," rebounded across the room like ping-pong balls. Following each testimony, the Relief Society president softly said, "Thank you for your testimony, Sister Smith."

After about thirty minutes of this, I made a decision. A testimony is found in the bearing of it—right? This is a missionary's mantra. Time to practice what I had once literally preached. I would say the right words, and maybe while I was speaking, something would change. I would be transported back to where I had been a year before. Here was my opportunity for a miraculous experience.

I nervously stood up and said, "I want to bear my testimony. I know that I have felt strongly about Joseph Smith in the past."

Avoiding eye contact with those around me, I continued, "I know I've had spiritual moments where my feelings told me that he was a true prophet. Well, I also know that he was a polygamist with more than thirty wives, and Emma didn't always know what was going on. He married a girl who was fourteen years old. I know a lot of the stuff he prophesied didn't happen."

I glanced around the room, naive enough to hope I might see some disembodied angel. There was no spirit, only the eyes of every woman in the room, staring at me with barely concealed shock.

Speaking more quickly, I continued, "But even if all of that is true, I still know he was a prophet because I had a good feeling about it before, so that feeling must still be true. And so I want to bear my testimony... because if I felt a feeling, which I was told was the spirit, then it must mean it's true. Right?"

My voice broke as I whispered, "In the name of Jesus Christ, Amen."

I sat back down and took a breath. A few women looked upset or flustered. Though we had all agreed to talk about Joseph Smith, there was a silent and absolute consensus in the room and in the church dictating what the conversation would include. Polygamy wasn't on the list.

After an eternity, the Relief Society president stood up and launched into her own testimony. She didn't thank me like she had the other women. She gave an impassioned testimony, and it had all the right things. Other women stood up after her, sharing faith-promoting words and stories. No one acknowledged anything I had said in their testimony. I was entirely invisible.

But the frosty judgment of the women in the room felt unimportant compared to the hope that I would feel some shred of goodness. I took a chance and bore my testimony. Now, I would find my faith again. Minutes passed, and I searched my heart, craving an irrefutable sign to return my testimony.

Instead of a burning in my bosom, I felt dread and disgust. This feeling had been brewing since I stepped through the church threshold, and now it was overpowering. Rather than finding my testimony, I only felt that I had lied. I stood up and lied through my teeth. I didn't believe in Joseph Smith. What's more, I didn't believe in The Book of Mormon, in the spirit, or even in God.

Before the meeting was over, I stood up and walked out of the room. No one stopped me or followed me out. My feet carried me to the car and away from that horrible, gnawing feeling. I sat there with my arms crossed, waiting until Jackson was finished with his Priesthood meeting. At home, I placed my leatherbound scriptures in a box in the closet. That was the last time I went to church. It was three months since I had started openly questioning my faith, and I was finally ready to act.

Later in the evening, I called my parents and told them my decision: I would no longer go to church. They knew I had been questioning for a while, and I finally felt it was time to break the news. I didn't consider myself Mormon anymore. I was done. In Chapter Three, I dive more deeply into these conversations and the planning I put into sharing this news.

Jackson told his family soon after. While my parents were sad, they were both very loving and understanding. I was incredibly grateful that I would still be able to call them and talk with them. I would still be in my mom and dad's lives, even if the church was no longer in mine.

My final attempt at faith was fruitless. These types of experiences are typical for Exmormons. Jackson recalls sharing his "Exmormon testimony" with our bishop when he called Jackson to his office to ask about his concerns. Another friend recalls peppering senior missionaries with questions about early church history, even though he ultimately knew they wouldn't have answers.

Exmormons initiate these final attempts because they often believe faith is still possible. Many people have a last, earnest attempt at faith before ultimately deciding to leave. Like the grand finale on the Fourth of July, this attempt is often monumental and looms large for the person who lost their faith.

Bearing my final testimony in Relief Society was terrifying, but the feeling of repulsion is impossible to forget. Without that experience, I may still wonder if there was anything more I could've done to save my faith. Saying the words aloud in a room full of members and in front of a photo of Joseph was my most clarifying moment.

If here in Chapter Two you are still feeling a large amount of indecision about your testimony, I suggest you initiate your own grand finale. Find a way to lay all your concerns on the table. Bear your testimony again. Reconnect with an old mission companion and explain every aspect of your struggle. Share a candid conversation with a bishop. Post a rant on social media. Allow yourself to ask all the questions you always buried deep inside.

You may find yourself 95% sure you want to leave the church. If this is you, ask yourself, "What do I need to do, say, or experience to clarify that final 5%?"

WHERE TO GO FROM HERE

You've had your crisis of faith. Your shelf finally broke under the weight of experiences and doctrinal concerns. Maybe your shelf cracked and broke after one late night of Googling and reading online. Perhaps it broke after years and years of small experiences, and finally, a straw broke the camel's back.

After the faith crisis comes something just as scary: what will you do with this newfound realization? After the dust settles and the shelf lies broken on the floor—what comes next? Do you take off your garments then and there? Do you text your bishop and let him know that you can't give your talk during sacrament meeting after all?

You find yourself now where I was then. You are on the precipice. No one else can decide for you. Many people have a crisis of faith and decide to stay in the church, whether wholly or partially. Some people stay for loved ones and for the community. I met many people like this on my mission. People didn't want to get divorced, so they attended every Sunday. Others were afraid of letting down close friends and family. Some people stay, still hoping to regain their testimony.

Staying in the church while not believing can be very enticing. After building a whole life around the church, leaving often means damaging relationships and destroying bonds. I wouldn't personally judge anyone for staying in the church while not having a testimony. When first confronted with the reality of leaving, I also wanted to keep it a secret. I entertained the idea of pretending to attend for the sake of family and friends.

If this is the path you choose to take, I encourage you to appraise whether this choice will be livable for you long term. How long and how much are you willing to keep up a faithful narrative? When played out, most people find that faking your way through life in the church will almost surely be more painful than being honest with your family and friends.

Yes, it is tremendously scary to share such massive, earth-shattering news with your family. It may mean some relationships cease. It may mean divorce. This is an impossibly difficult decision. Once you open your mouth and speak those words, your life will change.

REFLECT AND WRITE

- What do you fear will happen if you are honest about what you believe or don't believe?
- Can you conceal your true self from the people closest to you? How will it feel to be dishonest about your true convictions with your spouse, parents, and friends? Are you willing to prioritize other people's versions of who you should be over the chance to explore and discover your true self?
- What would a lifetime of participation in the church cost you?
- Are you willing to hide all activity not authorized by the church? This means concealing anything from drinking coffee to a potential relationship with someone of the same sex. This means lying about participating in Sunday activities that are not approved. This means foregoing a tattoo or hiding any alcohol when your family comes over.
- If you do not believe but want to stay in the church, are you still willing to continue to wear garments daily, hold a calling, go to church every Sunday, attend the temple often, bear your testimony, give church talks, and pay 10% of your income to the church as tithing?
- How close can your relationships with loved ones stay when you must hide every step you take outside of what a good Mormon should do?
- Will you bless and baptize current or future children into a church you do not believe is the truth? Or lie to family about a baptism taking place that never happened? Will you send your children away for a two-year mission when you believe the basis of the gospel is false? Will you lie about their temple marriage, too?

While you decide how to move forward with your faith crisis, know that you must live in the life you create. If you continue in the church after losing your faith, it may mean giving up large parts of yourself to keep the peace. It will also mean giving up the experiences and the self-discovery contained later in this book.

My advice? Rip off the bandaid. Keeping the peace in the short term will mean giving up yourself and your life in the long run. Choose yourself. Choose the freedom to do and speak who you are and what you feel without apology. Allow yourself to walk away from a toxic belief system rather than continue offering your life to the Mormon church. Yes, it will be challenging in the short term, but in the long term—you will thank yourself.

Once you know you no longer believe in the church, what will you do? Once your shelf drops, you will feel the need to make a decision. Will you leave the church, or will you stay in the church? Or will you try and do something in between—leaving the church spiritually and emotionally but continuing to attend for the sake of others?

Think of what will make you the happiest and the most fulfilled. Choose the life path that *you* want. Steer away from allowing fear to make this choice for you. The church rules so many choices and thoughts. Stepping beyond the bounds of this safety net will surely be scary.

The church tells you exactly who to be and how to act to be successful. If none of it is true, you're left with a completely blank slate. Blank slates are exciting but also very scary. Safety is knowing the exact path to follow for success and happiness. The church has provided that path your whole life.

REFLECT AND WRITE

Choosing how to move forward after losing your faith is incredibly challenging. Each step matters. You worry you'll lose everything if you make a wrong move. The fear of change is often much worse than the change itself. The decision to leave the church is deeply personal. You may make this choice quickly or over many years.

- Think of someone you trust with whom you can be honest about your faith crisis. Make plans to talk with them and get advice.
- Evaluate your mental health. Do you have decreased energy or happiness since beginning your faith crisis? Do you feel anxious if someone asks you about a change in faith? Seek out a faith-neutral counselor and talk it out. Many people are hesitant to try mental health counseling, but it can be massively helpful when going through a significant change.
- Look beyond this moment. Picture yourself at ages 25, 45, and 65. What will you want your life to look like when you are that age? What do you want to be able to say you've done with your life? How can you ensure you'll be proud of your choices now?
- Set a deadline. If you're having difficulty deciding to stay or leave the church, you may try setting a deadline. Sometimes, this forces us to consciously think about a big decision rather than waffling back and forth. Or this one may bring more anxiety. Choose this approach only if it works for you.
- Set aside time daily to write, think, and research your decision. Allow yourself space to mull over your choice. Move forward with purpose, and don't shove aside uncomfortable feelings.

When I left the church, I lost many friends. No one was ever outrightly rude to me or unkind. Many people stopped talking to me. After a long year and a half LDS mission with many companions and many close relationships, only one person continued responding to me after I left. Anyone who is no longer your friend because you left the church was not a friend to begin with.

CHART YOUR PASSAGE

The best part of leaving the church is choosing where you fall on this long Exmormon spectrum. You define your relationship to your past Mormon self and beliefs. Decide what those beliefs look like from day to day, week to week, and year to year.

On the following page is a graph to help you visualize where on the spectrum you fall. When I first was leaving, I was still somewhat spiritual and pretty socially Mormon. Now, I hover between socially progressive and atheist. You are allowed to decide. And you are allowed to change your mind.

Consider where you fall on this graph. Mark a dot in the area where you currently exist. Next to the dot, write the date.

You are allowed to slowly fade away from the church in a non-confrontational way, or you can go down swinging. Be an Exmormon missionary and post the *CES Letter* on your social media daily, or quietly exit through the back door to your new life. You are officially the master of your soul.

Write your reasoning for placing your dot where you did. Later in the book, you'll be reminded to revisit the spectrum to see where you stand. Take stock of who you are and where you are currently. When you look back on this phase of your life, it will help you remember and understand the choices you made.

SOCIAL AND RELIGIOUS SPECTRUM

	Very Religious Belief in God Attend church Daily prayer and study	**Spiritual** Belief in a higher power Live by spiritually-motivated guidelines	**Atheist/Agnostic** No belief in God Life is not impacted by belief in a higher power
Socially Mormon Sabbath worship Word of Wisdom Law of Chastity			
Average No Sabbath worship Moderate alcohol R-rated movies			
Progressive Politically outspoken Explore drugs and sexuality Tattoos and piercings			

REFLECT AND WRITE

- ✦ Where on the chart did you place yourself? Explain.
- ✦ Where do you think you'll place yourself five to ten years from now? Explain.
- ✦ What message would you share with your future self coming back to reflect on this self-analysis?

A note: The remainder of the book assumes you've more or less passed through the initial faith crisis and are ready to answer the question: *now what?* This does not mean you should stop reading if you're still not sure. Only that I'll be changing the language to be more absolute.

As I've stated several times, leave the church at the pace you feel is best—or don't leave at all. However, to stay true to the book's title and its mission, expect the remainder of the book to be devoted to instruction on leaving the Mormon church behind and entering a new, full life.

THREE
PROCLAIM
Boldly Be

We are all of us more complicated than the roles we are assigned in the stories other people tell.

—Tara Westover

As a member, the phrase "falling away" often crossed my mind. This is the process by which active, Jesus-loving members stop attending church. The lore shared by missionaries and members describes a family skipping church one Sunday. Then maybe the family decides it's "okay" to watch an R-rated movie. It's only a matter of time before the parents divorce, the son is gay, and the daughter is pregnant.

I completely believed in the slippery slope narrative: one wrong step, and you lose your faith and leave the church. The devil is in the details. It was impossible to imagine that a temple-attending, tithe-paying, Book of Mormon-reading member could wake up and stop attending church. Surely, a combination of laziness, Satan, and slow degradation of morals was the only explanation.

My mom would often share a story from General Conference. There was a woman who was a perfect saint but still drank coffee. The saint expressed, "The Lord will not keep me from heaven for drinking coffee."

Mom warned, "Even though the Lord probably didn't keep her from the Celestial Kingdom for her coffee drinking, all of the women's children eventually left the church."

The message was clear: a single chip in the perfect Mormon armor could easily lead to horrendous spiritual impacts on you or your family.

Once I experienced a loss of faith, I realized there was no such thing as "falling away." After a full-time mission, faithful temple marriage, and an entire lifetime of active church membership, I did not simply stumble and trip off the cliff of belief.

Throughout my faith crisis, I was reading scriptures and whispering prayers constantly. I held a calling and attended endowment sessions. I practiced my Mormon faith vigilantly, even as I was losing it. I did not slowly dissolve away from the church because I didn't wear garments while exercising or because I started drinking caffeine.

I left the church because the truth claims of The Church of Jesus Christ of Latter-Day Saints are false. The Book of Mormon is not the word of God. Heavenly Father, Jesus Christ, and the Holy Ghost do not exist. I no longer believe in the fundamental premises of the church. None of that has anything to do with the temptation to sin. It has nothing to do with the desire to drink or go to the lake on a Sunday afternoon. This narrative protects the church because it reinforces the idea that the church is *always* true and there will never be any "good" reason to leave.

After I lost my faith, I was maddened by how the portrayal of "falling away" benefits the church. Leaving quietly allows active members and leaders to stay in the land of cognitive dissonance. Disaffected members must remain silent while active Mormons freely fill social media feeds with conference quotes and videos from LDS.org.

My sister left the church a year before me, and the private gossip among the faithful was always about how she was "tempted away" from the church by an exciting new relationship. Someone told me, "The light has left her eyes," after my sister posted a photo of her engagement online. During Relief Society, one woman in my ward confided, "That will never happen to you, Alyssa."

I did not want to leave quietly. I did not want to start posting photos of me in a bikini on social media and have members say, "Look at her... falling away." As I left the church, I decided to share my decision with everyone I knew. I wanted control over my story. My life belonged to me. I wanted to clarify I did not fall away—rather, I stood up with eyes wide open and walked purposefully out of the door.

This is a paraphrased version of my social media post on September 10, 2017.

"This last year has been a transitional year for me. And despite how many times I rewrite the opening sentences of this post, there's no easy way to explain the change. I no longer believe The Church of Jesus Christ of Latter-Day Saints is the right path for me. I realize how disappointing this news will be to so many people love and respect, but I truly and completely believe I need to change my direction.

"I know every individual must come to terms with how they approach their beliefs. This was an incredibly hard decision and only came after months of searching and praying. This was not a choice from a desire to sin—to break the word of wisdom or to use Sunday as a second Saturday. This was not a decision that happened because I was offended or because I never had a testimony or a firm faith.

"This decision was born from a complete commitment to truth, myself, and God. After struggling for almost a year, I determined a decision needed to be made. After a long fast, committed thought, and focus, I decided the LDS church was not right for me.

"Many may feel I'm making the wrong decision, and some will feel it is for the best. I do not seek others' approval or disapproval; it is a completely personal choice. My choice comes from within—not from any external source. This is the right decision for me, and it is a choice I actively and decisively make."

Just as I proclaimed my faith loudly as a member, doing the same thing when I left felt appropriate. I'll note I posted this online several months after I told my news to everyone close enough to deserve a one-on-one conversation.

I am not suggesting this is the right way to leave or to share your decision with your circle. Many people feel the best way to leave is to share their decision with a few people or with no one at all. Depending on your experiences in Mormonism, you may have many people and groups with whom you feel you'll need to share your news.

Each person or group may require a different approach. As I've spoken with various people who have left the church, there are several prevailing categories of "leaving."

As I shared, my style was to leave loud and proud, but this approach may not work for you. What category fits you best? Which approach will help your parents understand? How can you best share the news with your non-member friends? Don't rush yourself into breaking the news before you are ready. Take your time to choose the best way to share your news with the people in your life.

Once your shelf falls, the first thought to bubble up is usually, "How do I tell my family?" The prospect can be intimidating, but trust the people who love you most in life will be there to support you. Extend grace when your family is surprised or needs time to process, but approach sharing your news with positivity and trust.

REFLECT AND WRITE

- Do you know anyone in your life who already left the church? How did they communicate it with those around them? What can you learn from their experiences?
- What are your biggest concerns when sharing the news with others? What steps can you take to protect yourself against heartache?

DISAPPEARING ACT

If you dislike confrontation, this could be the best approach for you. It may be easiest to time your faith transition with another change in your life—like moving to a new apartment, going away to attend college, or starting a new job or relationship.

Once you move, it's easy to disappear. No one in your new ward knows you. You could also simply stop attending and stop responding to calls. A simple text to your bishop, "We've decided to stop attending church," may be enough to exit. However, this approach may be tricky if you live in Utah or down the street from your very active family members.

Feel free to come up with various excuses to make this approach work:

"My job says I have to work on Sunday, so I can't attend."

"I can't hold that calling because I've already committed to my daughter's Wednesday night soccer practice."

"I've been feeling unwell lately and need to take Sundays to rest at home."

"I am visiting a friend, so I will be attending a different ward for a while."

Remember, you don't owe anyone anything. Your faith (or lack thereof) is no one's business but your own. If you choose to lie, conceal, or redirect questions—I am here to give you permission to say what you need to say.

While this quiet approach may work for friends and acquaintances, it may be a harder sell for immediate family who live nearby. You can only use excuses for so long. If you have a family member who will not allow you to leave quietly or disappear, maybe the following approach will work for them.

SLOW BURN

For a true believing member, it's impossible to believe someone could leave the church for a "good" reason. As a missionary, as long as investigators went to church three times, I was allowed to schedule a baptism. These three-week conversions were always viewed by members as "miraculous" and celebrated as if the convert had walked on water.

Imagine if your family accepted your choice to leave after only three Sundays' of introspection. Not a chance. Mormons love a good overnight conversion story but completely reject an overnight loss of faith. Go figure.

An easier pill to swallow is if your "deconversion" drags on for a very long time. One friend moved away from her home ward and family to attend a state college. Even though she stopped attending immediately, she knew her family wouldn't accept such a sudden departure. After about a year, she offhandedly mentioned, "I don't have many friends in my ward."

Another year passed, and she shared, "Work is hectic, so some Sundays I stay home and read my scriptures."

After another six months, "I only go to fast and testimony meetings these days."

After another two years, "I don't go to church anymore."

It may seem extreme to drag it out this long, but this made the most sense for my friend. She never argued with her parents on the phone or had to defend her choice. It was so gradual; there was never a moment for confrontation.

For some parents, children leaving the church feels like a death in the family. Going from active member to non-believer in one phone call can be quite a shock and could cause arguments and significant pain. Loved ones may be able to cope more easily if there is a lot of time to come to terms with the new reality. It also aligns with the "falling away" narrative the church teaches about less active members. While this might not be the reality for your loss of faith, it may be easier for your family to adapt to and understand.

CHRISTMAS AND EASTER MORMON

As the name suggests, these people only practice their faith on major holidays. Faith is more cultural than belief. If you are worried about the fallout if you leave the church outright, you may pretend for the most important days of the year.

Many people who are cultural Mormons fit into this category as well. A religious parallel to this approach is Reformed Judaism. These believers are less focused on observing rigid and traditional Jewish customs. Instead, they focus on the religion's cultural, social, and communal aspects. Essentially, they keep the community and let go of much of the dogma.

Many Utah Mormons practice in a similar way. Maintaining your membership in the church where most of your neighbors are Mormon is almost more convenient than leaving. Cultural Mormons keep the community and the culture while enjoying the occasional R-rated movie and cup of coffee.

In high school, I helped fellowship a less active family who fit this description. They would come to church every other month or so. The family became more active when the children were nearing eight, and the dad baptized all four of their children. One day, when I was at their house, the Relief Society dropped off dessert. After they left, my friend picked up a sprinkled sugar cookie and laughingly said, "I love less active cookies!"

At the time, I was shocked to realize how aware this friend was of the continuous overt fellowshipping of the ward. My friend was so comfortable, and maybe even happy, to exist in a Mormon middle ground.

One friend still wears garments when she travels home to visit family. Another friend borrowed a temple recommend and used it to see a sibling get married. This helped him avoid questions about why he was not temple-worthy. You may still attend your home ward and pray over dinner with your family, then go home and return to your irreligious ways.

While it doesn't always feel good to pretend, it may be the best option for those looking to avoid family drama or those who want to maintain friendships within a Mormon community. Use this if you haven't decided if you want to leave the church or if you want to stay.

BAND-AID RIP

You know what this means. Come out and say it. No dragging feet or twiddling thumbs—tell the truth, the whole truth, and nothing but the truth. Being honest can be terrifying, but it can also be unimaginably liberating. The longer you drag out the process, the more you prolong your emotional turmoil and pain.

If you want to perform the bandaid rip, I suggest writing a script, or at least a bulleted list, of what you want to share with your loved one. This will help you stay true to your resolution to be honest, clear, and to share everything all at once. Deliver your complete message during the conversation.

When sharing your news concisely, allow plenty of time for processing and questions during the conversation. Don't rush to get it over with; this will make it feel like a hit-and-run. Be direct while maintaining empathy and understanding. Offer them support if they need it and if you have the emotional availability.

While the bandaid-rip approach is intimidating, it is probably best for your mental health. Concealing the truth means protecting your loved ones from pain. It also means holding onto something painful and bearing the weight alone. When you prioritize the emotional needs of others, you may have to forego your own mental health.

For those who have the fortitude and strength, be straightforward and honest. Share your news directly and share the complete message. It may be appropriate to emphasize that your decision is final, as I did in my social media post. Being explicit about this lessens the opportunity for someone else to try and push you back into "slow burn" territory. Rip off the bandaid and give that wound the air it needs to heal.

EXMORMON ZEALOT

Not many people opt for this approach, but sometimes people come out with guns blazing. This scorched-earth mentality may end up damaging or ending some relationships, but sometimes, standing on a mountain and yelling the truth can feel amazing.

As a Mormon, I always considered myself a "member missionary." I've passed out hundreds of copies of The Book of Mormon and shared my testimony with countless people. As someone trained to share my beliefs with everyone I meet, it was hard to turn the urge off as I left the church.

I wanted to tell people about the similarities between The Book of Mormon and View of the Hebrews. I wanted to talk about polygamy in heaven. When I moved to New York, I would have long conversations over drinks with people about temple clothes and secret handshakes. It felt like removing the poison from my body.

When I left the church, I felt angry and jaded. I spent years and years in the service of a multibillion-dollar, racist, and sexist corporation with no truth. After giving and giving so much, I am not ashamed to say I still feel angry when I think about it. I will never get those hours and days and years back.

It feels good to share a post arguing against the church's stance on LGBTQIA+ marriages. I feel vindicated in sharing my feelings about early church history and equality for women. All disenfranchised members will never have any recompense. And so sometimes, when you're wronged, it can feel right to spread the word about a damaging organization.

These broad categories can help you consider different strategies for sharing the news with family and friends. I initially used the "slow burn" strategy, but now that I'm writing this book, it seems I've transitioned to "Exmormon zealot."

Use whatever strategy feels the most useful at the moment. Be honest with some friends and conceal the truth from others till you're ready. This is your life and your story. Share it in whatever way is best for you. When you are planning, remind yourself that these people love you. Love is powerful, and for most people, love stays true despite a religious change.

REFLECT AND WRITE

- ✦ Write the names of those you want to tell. Write how you plan to share the news.
- ✦ Compose a script. Plan the words you will use to share your decision with family, friends, and others. Remember, you do not owe an explanation to anyone; sharing the news can be enough.
- ✦ Plan your setting. Where will you tell them? Choose somewhere calm and quiet where you can focus on the message.
- ✦ Think of someone who can support you when you share the news with your family. Let them know beforehand and ensure they are available to talk or help you decompress after you share the news.

The thought of telling people news like this is usually much scarier than the actual experience of telling. Prepare for the worst, but know you can also hope for the best. Sharing personal truth with the ones you love most may be a moment of great strength and clarity. You are sharing difficult news, but it is okay to hope your family is loving and accepting.

These strategies can work well with extended family or friends, but some relationships, like your spouse or kids, require more consideration and planning. While you may be able to conceal your lack of church attendance from your parents, you can't hide much from your spouse. In the next sections, you'll find an outline of how to navigate sharing the news with different, closer relationships in your life.

MARRIAGE BELIEF DIVIDE

Fortunately, I had a spouse ready to exit the church within months of my faith crisis. Though I brought up my faith struggle first, Jackson was completely done with the church first. I was indecisive and continued to process the decision for three to four months. The weeks we were not on the same page caused me a lot of anxiety and heartache and left me worrying about outcomes if he left and I chose to stay.

Relationships vary widely, and most people can already guess how the people they live with will react to a faith crisis. Growing up, Jackson split time between divorced parents. His mom left the church when he was a toddler, so he always had a more nuanced view of church membership. Even when we were dating, it was pretty clear I was more devout. Between the two of us, I always brought up reading scriptures and attending the temple.

There was no way to hide my feelings from Jackson. Crying in his arms, I revealed I was questioning my faith within hours of admitting it to myself. His acceptance was immediate, and his love was unconditional. After that moment, we both started discussing the church all the time.

Between reading historical accounts, searching online, and sharing past experiences without a faithful filter, we both were ready to admit the church was not where we wanted to spend our lives. The faith struggle and subsequent exit from the church brought us closer than ever. A few weeks of difference caused me heartache. I cannot imagine the difficulty of having a split-faith marriage for years at a time—and possibly even a whole lifetime. Some can't make it that long, and some marriages end in divorce when one of the two chooses to leave the church.

One friend chose to keep her feelings to herself and continues to attend church as a quiet non-believer. Another friend wound up divorced after her faith crisis. Her spouse initiated the divorce within weeks of her sharing the truth, and they have three kids together.

This journey was heart-wrenching for her, but she shared how much clarity and freedom she has on the other side. When I asked her if there was anything she would have done differently in hindsight, she said, "I should've told him sooner and been more honest. I spent months locked in a mental battle with myself. Getting it over with was the most difficult part."

One of the most confounding aspects of leaving the church as a married person is how many values and promises in your relationship are tied up spiritually and culturally by the church. When one or both individuals leave all at once, all bets are off.

Within a Mormon marriage, there are countless cultural agreements. This list of understandings is so commonly understood Mormons never even discuss them. You never expect your Mormon spouse to do drugs, want an open relationship, get a tattoo, or want to try out gambling. Couples usually enter the relationship assuming the woman will become a stay-at-home mom and the husband will be the breadwinner.

When I married Jackson, I completely believed he would never smoke weed. After being out of the church for a month or two, he told me he wanted to try it out. This was earth-shattering to me. Not only because I had many negative connotations associated with using an illegal drug but because it also revealed something much more profound about our relationship.

I never expected him to smoke, and now he wanted to. What else did this mean? Would he want to waste all our money gambling? Would he still want to become a father? Would he end up cheating on me? The entire fabric of our relationship was intertwined with the values and morals set forth by the church. If some values unravel so easily and quickly, would the rest of our relationship soon be a pile of tattered shreds?

If you choose to leave the church while married or in a committed relationship, keep this in mind. You used to be a person—a Mormon— about whom your partner could make many, many assumptions. You are no longer that person.

Overnight (in the eyes of those around you), you have become someone who could transform into a polyamorous Democrat with no moral compass. You could murder your Italian lover. You could be gay, trans, bi, or nonbinary. You could wear a bikini to a family function. You could become a homeless addict. You could go topless at a beach or get drunk in a bar. You could pay someone for sex after attending a Pro-Choice rally. The pearl-clutching list goes on.

Be patient with your partner and with those around you. You know yourself, and you may feel that leaving the church simply makes you "not Mormon" anymore. As much as you can, learn how to be okay with being misunderstood. You may not be able to control what anyone else thinks of you or how they judge you, but you can control how you see yourself. Practice being comfortable with who you are and your choices. Communicate openly, but also try not to worry about what others think if you know you are making the choice you feel is best.

Even though you feel like basically the same person, your loved ones may react differently. Your family never expected you to leave the church, and then you did. When you show up to dinner in a tank top, it will feel shocking. They may wonder, "What other crazy stuff is yet to come?"

If you want to buy a coffee maker, donate to Planned Parenthood, or even try something even more staggering, be willing to open lines of communication. Before you make a choice outside the bounds of a Mormon "norm," talk the choice through with your partner. You do not need to ask for their *permission*, per se. Communicating versus getting permission for a choice are two separate things.

Over-explain and be extremely clear and specific. Remember it's okay to be misunderstood, and focus on being honest and open despite any judgment that may arise. Keep in mind these conversations are important even if *both* of you have left the church. Maybe one of you is okay with drinking alcohol, but the other isn't, for example. Losing your testimony doesn't necessarily mean you change your stance on drinking. Assume nothing about their stance on any "not-Mormon" church expectations or values.

Something like, "Hey spouse, I would like to try out coffee. I know I've never tried coffee before. How would something like that make you feel? Before I try it out, I wanted to see if you would be comfortable with my choice. Would you like to try coffee with me? Would you like me to try it when you're not around?

"I know this is a change from my choice as a member. How can I make this choice in a way that helps you feel comfortable? Do you have any questions?"

This is one example. You know your relationship, and you know your partner best. Honesty and abundantly clear communication is the best way to build trust. In the church, most of your behavior was assumed. In the first few months, and maybe years, out of the church, discuss everything.

As you begin to bend the rules of Mormonism, communicate any changes with your partner before you initiate. If your spouse comes home to a coffee maker on the counter, but you never discussed it, they will wonder what else about your relationship is going to change. However, if you always discuss before making a change in your life, your partner will feel more peace. Even if some behaviors may change drastically, at least they know you will address it with them first.

If your spouse draws hard lines on your behavior, it may signify a need to attend couples counseling. An ultimatum is a sign of an unhealthy relationship. If your partner says, "If you participate in X, Y, or Z, I will divorce you," then you probably need help discussing the complications in your relationship.

Leaving the church doesn't have to mean divorce or separation, but don't bury your head in the sand when situations like this arise. Seeking professional help may save your marriage. Jackson and I have attended couples counseling several times in our marriage. The result has always been closeness, better communication, and a happier home. You can even find Exmormon therapists who specialize in this type of faith transition online.

For most people, their greatest fear of leaving is how it will impact relationships with those around them. Allow time for yourself and for them to adjust. There may be tears and frustration. Remember, love and compassion can and will soften hurt feelings. Time will prove you're still more or less the same person after leaving the church, even if you show off those sexy shoulders occasionally.

SHARING YOUR DECISION WITH CHILDREN

Though it may not feel like it now, raising good and moral children outside the church is possible. Mormonism thoroughly convinces members it has the monopoly on raising kids correctly. During our faith crisis, I anxiously shared my hesitancies about raising kids outside the church with Jackson. I said, "What if we leave the church, and our kids become drug addicts?"

He solemnly responded, "What if we stay in the church, and our kids turn out to be gay?"

Programming members to assume it's impossible to raise happy and good children outside the church is just another form of brainwashing. Leaving with kids may mean being more purposeful in your parenting, but this is a good thing.

Have family dinner together every single night. Find playgroups and activities for your kids that reflect strong values. Read good books together. Talk to each other often, and about everything. Respect their viewpoints, even if they differ from yours. Encourage them to live in the way that makes them happiest, whatever that may be.

My friend Holly left the church when she was forty-five. At the time, she had a son on a mission and three teenagers in high school. I asked about what it was like to leave the church at this stage of life and how she shared the decision with her children. While I made up my mind over three months, she took years to decide. She did not want to move forward till she was absolutely sure the church was not true and she was making the right choice.

Though initially nervous to tell her kids, she knew it was a vital choice. She wanted them to know and understand, and she needed to be able to keep her family unit on the same page. When Holly finally broke the news, it was the most excruciating conversation she had ever had. Disappointing close friends and parents is brutal, but causing your own children such sadness is truly crushing.

All her children dealt with the news in their individual ways. Each child continued to attend church, and she drove them every Sunday. She fully supported their choice to continue practicing Mormonism. As they initially continued to attend church, they also listened to their parent's experiences and read the same books, articles, and information. Holly allowed the four to process the information and come to their own conclusion. Slowly, each began to understand their mother's choice.

Today, she has a strong relationship with her four adult children, and all free from Mormonism. After leaving, her kids also learned a lot about themselves and made the same discoveries all Exmormons make. One happily shared, "Mom, I realized I don't need to be Mormon to be a good person."

Our conversation ended with her sharing one of her greatest joys. When she is with her kids, every single person can be free to be whoever they want. Everyone can be their authentic selves—no one is faking or concealing anything.

Leaving the Mormon church when you have older children is a risk. When you leave, they might come to a different conclusion. However, the same principles apply. Don't live your life for anyone else, including your children. As you leave, your kids will be able to see your courage and resilience. You may also rescue them from spending a lifetime dedicated to Mormonism. Like many aspects of leaving the church, it will be hard but worth it.

LIVING WITH MORMONS

Being unapologetically yourself is nice and all, but if you're still living with your Mormon parents or family, it is much more difficult. The same goes for those currently attending a church-sponsored university. Many people experience a faith crisis when they depend on Mormons or Mormon resources in their day-to-day lives.

Consider your options and make decisions to protect yourself in the short term. If you feel your living situation may be in danger if you are honest about your faith, please wait to tell anyone. Do not risk homelessness or any form of physical or verbal abuse to be free of the Mormon church. If you suspect your parents may throw you out of the house if you tell them how you feel, wait.

In the meantime, work on making yourself as independent as possible. Get a job and save some money. Connect with people outside the church and try to grow a support network. Tell a counselor at school how you're feeling if you think they may be able to help. I am so sorry you are going through this, but I promise things will get better. Someday soon, you will be able to be free of the church—you only have to put up with it a little longer.

The same applies if you are attending a church school. Your bishop, professors, and the honor code office all have a seamless flow of information. My close friend was outspoken in the last semester of her four-year degree. She shared negative experiences in the church during one of her classes and in her ward. A few weeks before she graduated, BYU notified her she was expelled from the university.

BYU refused to grant her a degree after four years of study and work. She still does not have one today. Universities like BYU are much more insidious than you may think. Even sharing your faith crisis with a roommate could land you in the honor code office. It sounds ridiculous, but it's true. Your ability to graduate is connected with your ecclesiastical endorsement. Be careful who you trust.

If you're close to finishing your degree, go through the motions until you graduate. Attend church and classes, keep your head down, and get out of there with your sanity and your degree. However, you may have several years remaining before you can finish your degree. If this is the case, do your best to transfer to another university. Call a counselor at another university and ask them which credits transfer and how to get financial aid.

Take time to reflect on what is best for you and your well-being. Do what you must to protect your living arrangements, degree, and sanity. Once you are entirely independent, you can break away from the church. It will get better soon.

GRIEF IN ISOLATION

You are poignantly aware leaving the church is a scary and isolating experience. Discovering the reality of a faith that brought you joy and comfort is tragic. Letting go of Mormonism can be easy in some ways, but it is painful, too. I loved believing in a life after death. The idea of forever families is so comforting. Praying to a loving God brings confidence and solace.

Leaving the church and losing your faith doesn't simply mean you get a few hours back on Sunday; it means saying goodbye to everything you loved about the church, the community, and the gospel. You didn't stay in the church for as long as you did because all of it is trash. The church and the gospel are beautiful in many ways.

When you choose to leave, you will almost certainly experience pain, sadness, and fear. When I left the church, I realized I wanted to share my sorrow with my family members. However, my family found it difficult to support me. When I shared my choice, it felt as if there was only room for one person's grief within the conversation—and the room was not for me.

I hoped for comforting words like, "I'm sure it's tremendously hard to go through this change. How can I support you right now?"or "I want you to be happy," or "I'm glad you made the best decision for you," or "I am proud of you for living the way you feel is best."

Your family, parents, or spouse will also feel sad and confused when you share your decision with them but don't necessarily expect a shoulder to cry on. Family is often mourning the loss of who they hoped you would be. They may not be emotionally available to comfort you in your loss while dealing with their sadness.

Family also rarely thinks to ask the seemingly obvious question, "Why?"

In my experience, most members don't want to know what led you to lose your testimony. They may be afraid that the same information may also cause them to lose their belief.

It can be hard to manage the grief of others while not receiving support for your own sadness. After getting off the phone with my family, I felt even more alone. I lost God, and now it felt like I was losing my family. As you plan on sharing the news with your family and friends, I suggest finding support elsewhere to lean on through this process.

Schedule a session with a therapist the same day you plan to tell your family. Plan to meet up with a non-member or past member. Get dinner with someone who will emotionally support you after sharing difficult news. Plan on going for a nice walk, listening to your favorite music, or watching a great movie.

Make plans to protect yourself and to create space to grieve separately from your family. This will allow you to share your decision and talk it out with your family, and then process your grief later at another time if needed.

REFLECT AND WRITE

- What is one way you can take care of yourself during this difficult time?
- Who can you reach out to when you need help processing this change?
- Think of one thing you will miss about being Mormon. How can you create something new to fill the hole the church leaves behind? *Example: practicing meditation instead of praying*

KEEP LOVE AT THE CENTER

Sharing the news with your family is intimidating. After the initial faith crisis, it may be the most challenging part of the journey out of the church. If you fear sharing the news, remember your love for these people in your life. Hold this love close while you break the news to them. If there are unkind words or if there is judgment, try to let it slide off your heart instead of allowing it to root deep inside.

Your parents changed your diapers, fed you peanut butter and jelly sandwiches, and sat with you as you fell asleep at night. They've watched you grow from a tiny, sleepy baby into a complete adult with hopes and dreams. Your siblings remember water balloon fights and playing tag on the playground. These people we call family are precious, and they are flawed.

When you leave the church, you leave a massive community behind. And though that community is imperfect, it still may be the only community you've ever had. If at all possible, don't leave your family behind. Keep your Mormon parents and siblings as close as you can—or as close as they'll let you be.

There may be no eternity after death, but there is still love in this life to grasp onto. Hold it tightly. The church takes a lot from a person; don't let it take your loved ones—if you can help it. They may choose to cut you out of their lies, but if there's any chance you can maintain the love, I encourage you to try.

Your family are your people on this earth. Keep love at the center of these conversations. Remind your family often, "I love you. I appreciate you. Thank you for talking with me. Thank you for listening. Let's talk again soon." Maintain love and respect, and stay connected throughout this transition.

Sometime soon, you'll be on the other side of all this. Hopefully, it'll feel like very little has changed. Maybe there will be a few awkward moments, like when they go to a church service while you stay back or when you arrive with coffee in hand during Christmas. But ultimately, you're with family; you're with the ones you love. Even if it's a bit bumpy, at least you're on the roller coaster together.

FOUR

IDENTITY

Uncut Stone; White Canvas

What lies behind us and what lies before us are tiny matters compared to what lies within us.

—Ralph Waldo Emerson

The familiar face of a friend slid across my screen. She smiled cheerily, holding her three tiny children in her lap. Her husband sat behind her, his hands curling around her stomach: a pregnancy announcement.

Another baby? I thought to myself. *You've got to be kidding me.* The text beneath the post gleefully shared they were expecting their fourth. The post ended with a fervent testimony sharing the eternal importance of motherhood and forever families. An involuntary sneer crossed my face.

While I scrolled through her page, my son sat beside me, pushing his mini red Volkswagen bus back and forth across the tile floor. Smiling, I caught the bus and rolled it down the hall. He laughed and stumbled after it, then propelled it toward me again.

As we played, I relayed the baby news to Jackson. He responded diplomatically, "Your friend seems really happy. Of course, there's no way to know."

Of course, since leaving the church, I knew better. Turning my phone toward him, I showed Jackson the post. "She's *just* a stay-at-home mom," I countered, "Imagine being stuck with four screaming kids at home all day. Meanwhile, your husband gets to take hour-long lunches and contribute to the world."

Since leaving, it was nearly impossible to use the term "stay-at-home mom" without inserting the word "just" immediately before. The church thoroughly primed me to pursue a woman's God-anointed path. Somehow, every Young Women's lesson seemed to tie back to divine motherhood. My patriarchal blessing was more about motherhood than any other aspect of myself.

I refused to play this hand. Motherhood was the most insidious lie of traditional Christianity. Mothers are trapped by their children. Once they're conceived, your freedom disintegrates. The identity of motherhood is all-consuming, and once you walk through the door, you'll never break back out. While my son played, a work email popped up on my screen. "Do you mind if I respond to this?" I asked Jackson, walking toward the office door.

Fueled by my disdain for stay-at-home moms, I doggedly pursued becoming a mom with a stellar professional career. At the time, I was an assistant principal. This leadership position made me feel like I had conquered the world. Mornings began at 5:45 a.m. I usually walked back into the house after work at 6:30 p.m. The school where I worked was in utter chaos. Pandemic pandemonium and organizational disorganization made my job completely miserable.

When I looked in the mirror at the end of the day, exhausted, I told myself I was the happy one. "I am better than all my Mormon mom friends," I promised myself as I picked my son up from school, running on fumes, "I am a mom, *and* I have a career."

My superiority complex came from the conditioning I received at church. I was told all I would ever be was a mom. "You'll only need your degree if your husband dies," I heard more than once.

I felt so proud each morning when I walked into my office. When my paycheck hit the bank account, I had a vindictive urge to take a screenshot and send it to anyone who told me I would only ever be a mother. I was proving them all wrong, even if I was exhausted and unhappy at work.

As the school year wore on, my position at the school became more and more demanding. The hours somehow became even longer, and I began spending Saturday and Sunday working from home on my computer. In the evenings, I would hug my son on the couch. After a full workday, I had no energy for anything other than television. His hands were getting so big; he was somehow transforming from toddler to preschooler.

After my second son was born, I didn't go back to work. Looking down at his tiny little face, the war in my heart finally ended. A realization struck me—Mormonism was still dominating my choices. Instead of ardently following the church's teachings, I was now living to prove the church wrong. Either way, the church was still in control of my life.

Like a pendulum oscillating away from Mormonism, the powerful momentum pushed me to react in the opposite direction.

I hated the idea of being a stay-at-home mom because that is what Mormon women do. In reality, spending each day with my two children filled my heart with happiness. Loving motherhood made me human, and I couldn't allow my history in the church to steal one of life's greatest joys away from me.

As I continue to recover from Mormonism, I still see how my choices are often a reaction to my life in the church. I couldn't allow myself to enjoy motherhood on my terms. I had to prove something to myself and the people around me. I've finally found a way to embrace the parts of me that feel right, even if those parts are still so closely connected with what I learned as a Mormon.

My sons are still young. Someday too soon, they will go to elementary school and then on to middle and high school. Many years from now, they'll leave the house entirely. At some point, I'll go back to work. For now, I am blissfully content each morning as I make pancakes for my kids. Jackson took him to daycare, so I didn't see him till 6:30 p.m. on weekdays. Now, mornings are spent building Legos in pajamas.

Sometimes, when I am at a party or meeting new people, the old familiar question pops around the room: "What do you do?"

Everyone takes a turn answering, and when the conversation lands on me, I respond, "I'm a stay-at-home mom," attempting to speak confidently while avoiding the word "just."

I know someone in the room may secretly scoff at my response. There may be a woman who narrows her eyes a little and thinks, as I once did, "Imagine being stuck with two kids at home all day. Meanwhile, her husband gets to contribute to the world."

I understand her. I obviously was her. Disentangling myself from Mormonism is a never-ending process. Sometimes, I think a choice purely represents me and the essence of my being—then, in hindsight, I see I was motivated in response or reaction to my past. Who knows where a particular decision is sprouting from? We only know it feels right in the moment.

Mormonism had an iron grip on me and continues to play an undeniable role in my identity. You may feel you've left the church behind but then continuously find little bits and pieces of the church still spinning around in your mind. As you begin to take these first steps out of the church, move slowly and with purpose. Avoid being a pendulum: swinging quickly and mightily back and forth, constantly careening away or toward something—never peacefully centered.

A RIVER, NOT A BUCKET

You've gotten through your faith crisis in one piece. You decided to leave the church as a result of your faith crisis. You chose how to communicate the news to your family and friends. Okay, now it's time for some fun.

Examine the changing landscape of your mind. Many of your beliefs, guidelines, values, and assumptions about the world are now glinting in a different light. Some concepts and taboos may have already disappeared entirely. As you gaze around your brain, it may look completely foreign to you.

As Mormons, we are incredibly comfortable using the phrase "*I know*." We proclaim this turn of phrase loudly from pulpits in front of a few hundred people, "*I know* the church is true." *On my mission, I constantly said, "I know God will answer you if you pray."* Mormons *know* everything from the truth of The Book of Mormon to the reality of an afterlife.

After proclaiming "I know" for so many years, no longer knowing is terrifying. You may find yourself searching for something new to "know." I became convinced I had to hurry and choose the next thing to "know" as soon as possible. As if not knowing much at all was a moral failing.

Get comfortable with not knowing. Get comfortable believing one thing one day and then changing that belief the next. Today, you may think you'll never watch an R-rated movie or drink wine. Despite your current stance, a year from now, you may be sipping Cabernet while watching *The Godfather* without a second thought.

You are a human being in a constant state of flux, and that is *good*. You now have the freedom to change your mind. You have the liberty to evolve and change opinions when you hear new information. Instead of asking yourself, "What would a good Mormon believe on this subject," you finally get to ask, "What do I believe?"

I savor the ability to look inward for direction in life. Instead of processing every experience through the sieve of the church, I can finally use my own mind.

I can ask, "Do I want kids?" instead of, "I already know that a good Mormon woman should and will have children."

Now I think, "Do I like this song?" instead of, "Is this song what God wants me to listen to?"

Freedom to decide everything for yourself may feel scary. Freedom is intimidating because, at least with the church, you know the optimal path to take through life: blessed as a baby, baptism at eight, mission, temple marriage, kids, job, more kids, mission with your spouse, grandkids, death, eternal life.

Now, as a human being with no religion, you may realize that there are millions of paths your life could take. No kids? Pursue a nontraditional career? Have an OnlyFans? Travel the world? Move to a city and pursue your dream career? Stay single? Or you can still have kids, love monogamously, and live the same life you always planned—with a little more levity and caffeine.

When you're skydiving out of a plane, do you enjoy the feeling of weightlessness along with the view, or do you spend the entire time worrying about a failed parachute? For your sake, I hope it's option number one. You no longer have a proscriptive set of beliefs dictating your clothing, relationships, weekends, and money.

You get to choose it all. You're a kid at a candy shop with an unlimited budget. You're behind the wheel of a car with a full tank of gas and an open road. With no one to pray to, and no spirit to guide you, and with no church guidelines—who are you? The answer is that you are whoever and whatever *you* choose. Where will you go? *From now on, anywhere you want.*

Imagine a river rushing and winding through a forest. Teaming with life, the water dances over smooth rocks and grassy reeds. Take a bucket and fill it with water from the river. Can you point to the bucket and honestly say, "Look, here is the river." If you collected rocks or caught a fish, could you call them the river?

No—and why not? The river is a vibrant, complex system. You cannot identify it using parts, only through embracing its entirety. No one piece of the river is the river. A river is vast and changes from day to day and from hour to hour. No one person can know the sum of a river.

You are the river. As we attempt to label ourselves or others, it is like equating the bucket of water to the river itself. I am a mother, but I am also a writer, runner, teacher, and Exmormon. To pull one of these descriptions out as my single defining purpose or identity is idiocy, but we do it all the time. You are a vibrant, complex creature. I may want to shove my Mormonism deep into a black hole, but it is a winding, jade-colored tributary flowing into my sum total.

Mormonism brought me a husband I love. Considering my irreligious peers, it is unlikely I would've married at twenty-three without the church. He is the bedrock of my river. Mormonism instilled a love of children into my heart, and now I have two wonderful sons. Most of my friends don't have kids yet. This is not to make a value judgment, and being unmarried and childless is a great life path for many people. I just know Mormonism brought many good things into my life.

Disentangling the good and bad is one of the most challenging aspects of leaving. I hate the church because it made me hate my body. I love the church because it led me to a loving partner and two sons. No power on earth can remove my past from me. There is no way to know who I would be without Mormonism.

I cannot examine my soul in a vacuum. I can't know if who I am comes from my essence or if it is simply a compilation of experiences. Maybe without Mormonism, I would be a best-selling author living in a penthouse in New York City. I would have pursued writing sooner if not for the church and my father's blessing. Maybe without Mormonism, I would've died in a drunk driving accident after a high school party in Kentucky. Mormonism helped me avoid some bumps along the way.

This life I've lived means I can't piece out my "true identity." No one truly can. No human becomes an adult without being sculpted by family, friends, and culture. We're left with the unknowable river, and we're left with the present and future. As Heraclitus wrote, "No man ever steps in the same river twice, for it's not the same river, and he's not the same man."

The past is already sorted. Pull meaning and identity from the past, but don't allow it to stagnate your future. I often wonder, "Who would I be without Mormonism?" but I know I am asking the wrong question.

These types of *what if's* and *if only's* are a supreme waste of creative energy. Instead of wasting away your mind regretting the past, enjoy the present and prepare for the future.

Who do you want to be?

Where do you want to go?

What do you want to become?

As you survey the new landscape of your mind, explore who is under the hood of your skull. While it's almost certain you will continue to change and evolve as time passes, it is comforting and exciting to formulate new beliefs and meld old with new.

Try out answering some of the following questions before reading more. In leaving the church, you're removing a huge chunk from yourself. Rather than leaving a vacuum behind, plan to replace the old with an intentional new. Talk through these questions with a loved one or friend who supports your choice to leave, or journal and reflect alone.

REFLECT AND WRITE

- ✦ Do you believe in God? Jesus? The Holy Ghost? Why or why not?
- ✦ What values from the church do you want to continue to hold? What values will you stop observing?
- ✦ Do you want to stop attending church altogether? Are you interested in investigating different religions? Why?
- ✦ Write the name of someone you respect and admire. What about them inspires you? What values can you incorporate from their example?

FRAMEWORKS TO EXPLORE

After leaving the church, many different philosophies, beliefs, or frameworks are available to learn from and adapt to your life. Many Exmormons find that after deconstructing Mormonism, it's impossible to believe in anything else. The church dedicates significant energy to reasoning through why other religions are not "true." This leaves many feeling nothing is true after leaving the Mormon church.

That being said, there are several systems which are common new beliefs and frameworks for Exmormons. Even if you don't find a system as all-encompassing as Mormonism, studying new ideas can lead to a greater understanding of the self and the world around us.

As I've mentioned, I have slowly morphed throughout leaving the church. When I first left, I was more or less a nondenomina-tional Christian. I still tried to pray and believe in God, Christ, and the Holy Ghost. After a few months, I became more agnostic. I wanted to believe there was a higher power, but I felt it was not likely. After I was out for about two years, I became an atheist. This is where I reside today.

Time may still push me towards some other belief, and I'm okay with that. I am content with choosing what makes sense for me now but not swearing on it for eternity. After a lifetime in the church, I am now happy with changing my mind when confronted with new information.

Below are the most common beliefs I've seen others gravitate toward. During this time of indecision and searching, the best medicine is reading, learning, and opening your mind. There is so much value and beauty in the world outside of Mormonism. Fill the void Mormonism left behind with a new bounty.

OPTIMISTIC NIHILISM

This framework is my current landing pad. While I am an atheist in the sense that I don't believe in God, it wouldn't be my first belief descriptor. Atheism is a claim you *don't* believe in something.

Optimistic nihilism is a philosophy that life has no inherent meaning or purpose. Rather than viewing this as a negative, it encourages individuals to create their own motivation for existing. Since nothing in life ultimately matters in the grand scheme of things, we should embrace the freedom that comes with this realization and make the most of our lives.

This outlook appeals to me because I am happy and content even though I don't believe in God. Ultimately, I am only a buzz of molecules floating in space, which is made of other buzzing molecules. When I die, my body will go in the ground. In the expanse of the universe, my life is an infinitesimally tiny blip of nothingness.

For some, this may induce a feeling of existential dread, though it makes me feel free in a way I've never experienced. In Mormonism, every choice has eternal consequences. God tracked my every thought. My soul hung in the balance of every decision. Mormonism and my anxiety were truly best friends. Anything other than exact obedience meant I was betraying God.

Now, as an optimistic nihilist, I am free from eternity. This means I can enjoy the now and think nothing of eternal salvation. I don't want a planet or to become a god; I want to live my life and enjoy my family. Choosing my own path has been one of the greatest joys of leaving the church.

One of the primary benefits of optimistic nihilism is that it alleviates religious anxiety and pressure. There is no need to find and fulfill a predetermined purpose in life. Instead of feeling burdened by expectations or the fear of failure, create your own goals and meaning. Pursue what truly matters to you, unrestrained by dogma.

AGNOSTICISM, ATHEISM, AND SECULAR HUMANISM

Agnosticism is the view that the existence of God, the divine, or the supernatural is unknown or unknowable. Atheism is the lack of belief in the existence of God or gods. These beliefs are similar enough that they're in the same section, like two apples from the same tree.

Secular humanism is a stance that embraces logic, reason, and science as the basis for belief. It rejects any and all dogma, superstition, and supernaturalism as the basis for making decisions and living life.

After Mormonism, I can barely engage in a conversation about something like astrology because it feels like another religion. However, some of my closest Exmormon friends love using astrology to make sense of reality. Mormonism poisons the well for many Exmormons. Once you're out of the church, little withstands the scrutiny you developed while leaving the church. After the God of Mormonism falls, no god replaces him.

Atheism and Agnosticism mean no religious code or belief will dictate what you do and do not do. For those worried about this aspect of losing your faith, I offer this quote from Penn Jillette, "The question I get asked by religious people all the time is, without God, what's to stop me from raping all I want?

"And my answer is: I do rape all I want. And the amount I want is zero. And I do murder all I want, and the amount I want is zero. The fact that these people think that if they didn't have this person watching over them that they would go on killing, raping rampages is the most self-damning thing I can imagine."

As a nonbeliever, you have the freedom to live by the dictates of your conscience. For me, this means prioritizing my family, living a healthy lifestyle, and being kind and thoughtful to those around me. You can discover what it means for you.

MAINSTREAM CHRISTIANITY

Christians are those who believe in Christ, God, and the spirit. They believe in life after death, repentance, and the Bible. There are many different denominations of Christianity, and Mormonism is one of them. There is a lot of hope and comfort in believing in God and Jesus. Attending a church each week also provides a community of like-minded people. Past members who still believe in God and an afterlife might go "church shopping" to find a congregation and denomination where they feel happy.

Some members transition to the Episcopal church. Other past members like going to the Presbyterian Church. You may enjoy what my family called a "band church." These churches focus on community, loving those around you, music, and sharing non-denominal messages about faith and charity.

Past members may also still feel spiritually minded instead of religiously minded. If this is you, experiment with prayer and continue to read whatever scriptures you choose. Develop your personal relationship with God outside of a church building. You may be happy with simple prayer, spiritual contemplation, and consuming uplifting spiritual content on your terms.

NEW AGE SPIRITUALISM

Eclecticism is the number one marker of New Age Spiritualism. Rather than one core set of beliefs, this approach invites all forms of worship and belief. This framework focuses on holistic well-being, introspection, and personal growth. It encourages alternative healing methods and respect for nature.

Tarot cards, divination, crystals, and astrology all fall into this category. It is up to the individual to decide how to incorporate these ideas into their lives. Some may follow Wicca with a religious fervor similar to Mormonism, while others study it to learn history and nature-based spirituality.

Many of my friends use tarot—not to see the future—but to reflect. While pulling cards from a tarot deck, they might see some pattern. The pattern makes them think of something meaningful in their lives, like a frustrating work situation or a burdensome relationship. The tarot cards essentially hold a mirror to one's life and force introspection and consideration.

My friend, Levi, shared the following about tarot reading, "By highlighting unique, seemingly separate ideas all within a single context, you're likely to draw new connections, be more mindful, and provide yourself with answers you've been looking for.

"It reminds me of something I heard once about flipping a coin to make a decision. You assign one path to heads and the other to tails. Pay attention to what you hope for as you flip the coin into the air. Then, regardless of the outcome, choose the path you hoped for. The coin is a tool to help you be honest with yourself."

Women are more likely to practice portions of New Age Spiritualism, but these concepts aren't gender specific. My favorite aspect of this framework is the ability to fully adapt it in whatever form is most valuable to the individual. Cast spells at the summer solstice, use tarot for self-reflection or use crystal healing for a holistic approach to well-being. Practice whatever aspects of New Age Spiritualism bring you peace and goodness.

BUDDHISM AND EASTERN RELIGIONS

Buddhism is one of the world's largest religions and originated 2,500 years ago in India. Buddhists believe that human life is suffering and that meditation, spiritual and physical labor, and good behavior are the ways to achieve enlightenment or nirvana. Some Exmormons adopt Secular Buddhism into their lives. This means taking lessons from Buddhism without necessarily believing in all its religious tenets.

Fundamental beliefs include the principle that the self is ever-changing. There is no fixed, permanent "self." Rather than a journey to "find yourself," it is better to create the self you want to be in each passing moment. Another belief is that life is constantly in flux. This can help one to stay present in the moment instead of living in the past or future. Meditation is a key component of Buddhism and can be used as a secular version of prayer to achieve similar contemplative and stress-relieving results.

Buddhists follow the Novel Eightfold path. This approach leads to nirvana. The eight practices are right view, right resolve, right speech, right conduct, right livelihood, right effort, right mindfulness, and right samadhi. These aspects of belief help an individual achieve inner peace and better understand themselves and reality.

Eastern religions are quite different from Christianity, and the basic philosophies contain significant value. Much of the philosophy focuses on how to live in and understand current experiences. Rather than believing in an unseen God, there is a higher focus on the inner self. It provides a lens for experiencing life instead of a moral dogma to follow unquestioningly. It is usually not intended to be taken literally. Secular Buddhism also welcomes the use of science to understand the world around us rather than rejecting science when it is at odds with the Bible or other religious teachings.

Eastern religion is vast, and it is impossible to encapsulate every tenant of the belief here. However, from conversations with many Exmormons, it is a favorite new framework for understanding life and the human experience.

REFLECT AND WRITE

- ✦ What are the core questions or dilemmas I have about life, purpose, or existence that I'd like to address through a new belief system?
- ✦ How do I envision a fulfilling and meaningful life? What elements would it include?
- ✦ Think back to when you were fully in the church, and compare that person to who you are now. What is different? What is the same?
- ✦ Look to the future and to what new versions may be coming towards you still. Who do you see? Who will you be?
- ✦ What do you believe is the purpose of your life? What do you hope to achieve or find through this exploration of new beliefs or frameworks?

A CHANGEABLE VALUE SET

The belief sets outlined above are a few examples to explore. Investigate every belief and framework under the sun if you have the urge. Your beliefs have been limited to an extremely proscriptive religion. Refrain from sprinting from Mormonism to the next belief system as quickly as possible.

While investigating other belief systems, recognize many forms of belief are not meant to be taken to the letter. Though Mormonism should be taken as literally as possible, many beliefs are highly symbolic. I was raised to believe Noah's Ark's story occurred precisely as described. This caused a bit of confusion when I learned there's not enough water on the planet to flood every surface.

Worshiping Hindu gods with many arms or animal heads may seem unfathomably odd until you reconsider the purpose of gods, the value of worship, and the altruistic reasons for religion. Introducing a monotheistic tradition about a man who found a gold book in the woods may seem similarly bizarre to someone from India. Most religious beliefs seem peculiar unless we learn them from childhood.

Some people leave the church and immediately find a new belief system to join. This is the religious equivalent of looking for a rebound after a long-term relationship. Focus on the journey rather than obsessing over finding your next "true" religion. If something resonates, investigate more. Pick and choose. Change your mind. I've found tremendously more joy and growth from concentrating on exploration over destination.

As Exmormons, our minds are primed for belief. We want absolute truth. The church taught us if we lived a particular way and checked all the boxes, we would reach self-actualization. If we followed Mormon doctrine, we could be our best selves in this life and live in heaven with God in the next. That's a lot of certainty.

Don't jump into bed with a rebound religion. Resist the urge to settle into some new idea and proclaim, "Here it is! Now I've really found it!" The world is vast, and the possibilities are endless. Search for ideas that excite you and challenge you.

It may be too soon to move headfirst into a new belief system, but you start searching for an outlook that resonates. Here is a step-by-step process for sifting through countless options and beliefs. This is a method I used as I left the church.

REFLECT AND WRITE

1. **Reflect on current values.** Make a list of beliefs you still hold and beliefs that no longer resonate with you.
2. **Identify new beliefs.** Think of new ideas and standards you have developed since your faith crisis. Reflect on moments you felt strongly while reading a book or engaging in a conversation. Anytime you cross something that elicits a strong reaction, reflect on it. Why did you feel that way?
3. **Research and learn.** Read books. Listen to podcasts. Enjoy new music. Watch classic films. Talk with interesting people. Search for newness in the world. Find connection with a world outside the church. If a belief system rings true, study it even more.
4. **Evaluate.** As you encounter new ideas and philosophies, assess them against your current beliefs. Research and explore to discover if you want to add a new belief to your outlook. If something doesn't speak to you, that's okay. Search for a life outlook that is uniquely your own.
5. **Write.** Use this as a tool for reflection and self-discovery. You will learn more about yourself when you write your feelings and thoughts. I often end up editing, deleting, or rewriting as I write. This process adds clarity to your vision.
6. **Connect.** Talk with others who share your beliefs and principles. Find connection with a group or community that supports you on your journey. Look for people in your life who can listen and talk with you openly.
7. **Rinse and repeat.** Identities are ever-evolving. Use this framework again and again as you investigate new corners of what life has to offer.

IDENTITY AND COMMUNITY

Belief is the core of Mormonism. Doctrine is the gravity pulling each person to church every Sunday. When you lose faith, you stop believing in The Book of Mormon and Joseph Smith. But when you let go of your grasp of the religious dogma, a whole second aspect of your identity falls alongside it.

When we lose faith, we lose more than the teachings of Mormonism—we lose our cultural community, too. And in the same way you now have a blank slate to fill with new beliefs and outlooks, you may also be experiencing the need to find a new community outside Mormonism.

Most active Mormons are deeply ingrained in Mormon culture. As a child, I moved around a lot. Each time we moved, we always dropped whatever box we were unpacking to go to church. Between Helena, Montana and Frankfort, Kentucky, my only constant was the church and the members. My wards were often tiny, and there were very few members, especially compared to a place like Utah. Despite the small community, most of my closest friends growing up were always Mormon.

When I left the church, I left behind a belief system that permeated everything. And while losing my religion was at the forefront of my mind, I also had to grieve the loss of my community. Almost everyone I knew was a member of the church. While most of this chapter is dedicated to losing a belief system, it also seems necessary to include how to adjust to losing your community.

Identity is cultural and community as much as it is belief. One of the most empowering aspects of belief is how it connects you with others who see the world in the same way. As a member, you likely spent significant time with other members due to callings, temple trips, Sunday worship, and youth activities.

You also connect with members over the strict rules dictated by Mormonism. As an active Mormon, there will not be any late-night drinking at the bar with nonmembers. You will not meet new friends at a coffee shop. Members don't join organizations that meet on Sunday or require significant free time. Mormonism is so restrictive that most people end up forming relationships with people who follow the same strict rules. This is what builds the Mormon community and makes it so incredibly rock solid.

Certainly, you will keep some of your Mormon friends and family. Some members are very accepting and loving and will continue in a friendship regardless of an exit from the church. After leaving the church, I needed to search for new communities. Many member friends cut off contact once I left, but I was ultimately okay with their reaction to my departure.

After I lost my testimony, I didn't want to hang out at Linger Longers or church basketball games. Maintaining a relationship with a community brought together by a hurtful lie did not interest me. When I lost my faith, I felt isolated. I no longer connected to the community of my past, but I didn't know how to find and meet new people.

If you feel unmoored from your community, I understand you. The initial days and weeks after leaving the church can feel very solitary. You may feel isolated because your friends stopped talking to you, and you may feel lonely because you no longer connect with them, either. The good news is there are so many communities of people who are welcoming and kind. The challenging news is you have to do the work to find your new community and put in the work to connect.

After leaving the church, you'll no longer have a one-stop shop for friends, dating, babysitting, mentorship, and networking. Mormonism is great because the moment you move into a new area, you have a built-in community conveniently waiting for you. And even if you don't absolutely love your new ward, at least it's there.

The best things in life are not easy. Finding a community you love is more complicated than staying with the community you already know and understand but dislike. As an introvert myself, making new friends is daunting. Please, do not make your new community Netflix and Doordash. Do not burrow inwards in the absence of friends. Putting yourself out there is intimidating and tiring, but you can do this.

While there are many ways to find new friends, a perfect place to start is the Exmormon community. I've been out of the church for seven years, and most of my closest friends are Exmormons. Many of them attended BYU with me, and we left around the same time. There's something special about Exmormon friends. You understand each other in such a specific, satisfying way. You can finally rant about the temple, vent about silly rules, or drunkenly sing lines from primary songs together.

Finding Exmormons is pretty simple, at least in larger urban areas and anywhere in Utah. You may even be able to connect with Exmormon friends from your past wards who left before you. There are a lot of Exmormon Facebook groups, and you can post on the r/Exmormon subreddit to see if anyone is in your area. Exmormons also congregate on TikTok, and many creators will tag their location. Try sending a direct message to see if they can suggest a meetup or ask if they want to meet for coffee. In my experience, Exmormons always swing the door wide open.

While Exmormons make great friends, finding friends completely removed from Mormonism is also healthy. It's nice to meet people unfamiliar with Mormonism because you can explore who you are outside of the church. Talking with never-Mormons is also cathartic because they affirm how much your Mormon experience was utterly atypical. I'll never forget how fun it was to explain the endowment to a table of never-Mormon friends at a bar in New York City.

You can also seek out other communities that involve your interests and hobbies. Look for people involved in things you love; you'll have the perfect ground to build a relationship. These can be online communities or people who meet in person where you live. Volunteering, joining a book club, taking classes, and networking events are other ways to meet like-minded people.

Find ways to contribute to your new community. Bring a dish or a bottle of wine if you're invited to someone's home. If it's your first time at a book club, bring a few suggestions for next month's read. Before a networking event, brainstorm how to help others with their endeavors. Add goodness to the lives of others, and they will add goodness to yours.

Building a community takes time. Connecting with people outside the church is more challenging than walking into a ward for sacrament meeting, but it is infinitely more exciting. Be open to new experiences, and be patient when making new friendships. Actively seek out opportunities that align with your interests and values.

Most people understand leaving the church means losing your belief system, and you may naturally begin to look for new frameworks and beliefs to fill the hole. Explore the countless ideas in the world, but don't forget to find your new community. A community is how you find comfort after leaving the church. It's how you find support after so much loss.

FIVE

PAUSE

Slow Steps with Long Strides

The trail is the thing, not the end of the trail. Travel too fast, and you miss all you are traveling for.

—Louis L'Amour

The first time I got drunk was a disaster. Jackson and I had tried one bottle of wine the week before, and I could barely swallow three sips. The murky red liquid burned my throat. This was a month or so after deciding to leave the church; everything was very new. Jackson was out of town, and my friend, Anna, came to my apartment. She also recently left the church and was as curious and ignorant about drinking as I was.

We drove to the state liquor store in Utah, determined to buy whatever was needed to become inebriated. Walking through the aisles, I was immediately overwhelmed. After surveying the selection, we purchased a bottle of tequila, white wine, and a 6-pack of beer. We went home and carefully placed the different drinks down on the table.

With our goal to get drunk in mind, we started with the bottle of tequila. Shot glasses were an essential element of drinking in my mind; they were always present in the bar scenes of old Western movies I watched as a child. However, Jackson and I were so freshly out of the church that we had no appropriate glassware. My Mormon home had no wine glasses, beer steins, or shot glasses. Instead, we used measuring cups.

We choked down the first shot—which was probably more like two—and looked at each other. I waited a bit, then asked, "Do you feel anything?"

"No," she responded, and we both sat for a moment.

In my Mormon naivete, I thought when you drank, the effects were essentially immediate. After waiting for two or three minutes, we tried another shot. It was like drinking nail polish remover. I grabbed some Gatorade so we could wash the taste away. After a grimace and some dry heaving, the same conversation played over again. Neither of us felt any different.

Can you guess what we did next?

Thirty minutes later, we were more than halfway through the bottle of tequila. Thinking we must be impervious to the effects of alcohol, we decided to switch to wine. As I struggled with the corkscrew in the kitchen, Anna called out from the couch, "I can't feel my lips."

Suddenly, I realized my hands weren't cooperating as I attempted to unplug the cork. I sat down, and the room began to spin slightly. We both started laughing, red in the face, "I feel it now!"

The rest of the night is a blur. What started as fun quickly became chaos. I threw up in the toilet and was lying on the ground when I heard a loud thud outside the bathroom door. Anna cried, "My eye, my eye!"

She had tripped over a chair leg and hit her face against the corner of the kitchen table. We called Jackson and told him what was happening, voices slurring. "Are you okay?" he asked and sounded freaked out. I felt sick and began walking back to the toilet, hanging up without responding. I threw up again and fell into bed.

When I woke up the following morning, I had fifteen or so missed calls. Anna slept beside me on the bed, her left eye the color of a robin's egg. At some point in the night, I texted my extended family chat, "Wha arrue dg." My first ever drunk text.

After a lifetime of adamant rule-following, things can get hairy when the brakes come off. After a complete loss of personal identity, you have a meltdown waiting to happen. I felt such excitement and urgency to "be out of the church" that I sprinted toward all the experiences I had previously rejected.

During my time at BYU, I never attended a single party where there was alcohol present. My devout Mormon parents never drank. At 25, I had never stepped foot into a bar. In hindsight, that night drinking with Anna is both funny and scary. The charge to try out drinking was so enthusiastic it turned into a negative experience.

INTENTION AND DIRECTION

You were a Mormon. Then, you had a faith crisis. You probably had disagreements with family and friends when you shared you were leaving. There's a good chance you're experiencing thoughts and emotions in ways you never expected. Consider this a psychological firestorm. Move slowly. Move more slowly than I did, at the very least.

I've also seen friends go the other way—rather than sprinting, they freeze. The fear of life outside the church is potent. The path of least resistance is to live exactly as you did before, only without going to church. Some friends go years without trying coffee, wearing shorts in the summer, and having open conversations with family about faith transitions. For some, trying new experiences isn't exhilarating; it's terrifying.

You are the master of your soul. Maybe coffee isn't for you or a Mormon standard of modesty is how you're most comfortable. While there is one path to being a "good" Mormon, there are countless ways to be an Exmormon. You can still believe in God, keep the word of wisdom, or live your life in whatever other ways you desire. After a lifetime of following the rules of a rigid religion, give yourself permission to follow the path you feel is right for you.

Life is long. Whether your urge is to freeze or to sprint, taking time to move with purpose and intention is incredibly important. If you sprint, you may rush into decisions you end up regretting. If you freeze, you may find yourself in personal purgatory; you no longer believe in the church but haven't invited anything new into your life to fill the void. Neither is ideal.

Imagine you're preparing for a feast. This will be the most lavish and meticulously planned feast imaginable. You will need twenty years to prepare for this feast. It involves carefully designing a menu, sourcing ingredients from all over the world, and curating a guest list. You'll eat oysters from Prince Edward Island. A chef from France will fly in and prepare boeuf bourguignon. The water will be filtered from a spring in the wilderness of Southern Norway.

Every minute detail of this feast will need to be planned, from the exact temperature of the dining room to the color of each person's shoelaces. Not a single aspect will be forgotten; everything will be carefully contrived. Each year, you spend hours and hours getting ready for this one single day. Your mind is constantly fixated on this extraordinary night of perfection.

Finally, the day of your feast arrives. The table is flawlessly set, and each guest is in their place wearing the finest clothing. Amber light glints off the immaculate silverware and the first dish is placed before you. You pick up your fork and take the first bite—but something is off. In the years spent planning for this one night, there is one thing you forgot to consider:

You have no idea how to sit and enjoy a feast.

So much time was dedicated to planning and preparing for the future that you never figured out how to relish the moment. Your mind was always focused forward; the present was always cast aside. And just like that, the feast is over, and the moment is gone in a flash. You did not have the capacity to appreciate the feast that took you years to plan.

Humans plan a lot of feasts. In high school, we look forward to college. In college, we dream of our first real job. When you're dating, you wonder when and if you'll marry. Once you're married, you think about kids or a bigger house. When we're eating lunch, we ponder on what's for dinner. Happiness is always hiding beyond the horizon line.

We tell ourselves: *once I get there, I'll be happy, important, or special.* Usually, once we arrive, we look around and realize "I still don't feel complete." Finding joy in the moment and being present sometimes feels impossible, especially when leaving the church.

Learn to enjoy the feast. Take as much time as you can to ease into the newness. Taste and savor each moment. Happiness and greatness are not at some distant and far away place—let it be here and now.

ALIGNING ACTIONS AND VALUES

Reading this book is a wonderful place to start. Embrace the mindset of "one step at a time." You can take those steps very slowly; when you turn around, you'll have come a long way. If you have the desire to try something new—something previously discouraged by the church, use the outline on the next page.

Following these steps will make it much easier for you and your relationships. It will also help you stay safe while trying new experiences. The church wasn't all wrong when warning against certain substances and activities. New sexual experiences can put you in danger. Trying drugs without any education can be hazardous to your health.

1. **Research, learn, and plan.** How does it work? What are the risks? What are the rewards? Watch YouTube videos, listen to podcasts, and read articles. Consider the setting where you want to try out this new thing. Set a day and time when you want to experiment.
2. **Discuss with a trusted and open-minded friend.** Express your desire to try out something new. Ask their advice and see what tips they may have. If you don't have a friend you trust, you can ask for advice on the Exmormon subreddit.
3. **Share your decision with others, if needed.** If you're in a committed relationship, it's best to communicate before acting. You may need to tell your parents, depending on your age. This is not to get permission, necessarily. In many cases, significant changes are easier to swallow when communicated first. The more communication, the easier the change is on the ones you love.
4. **Sample, then reflect.** Try one cup of coffee. Get a consultation at the tattoo parlor without getting the actual tattoo. Say "fuck" out loud when you're alone and see how you feel. More examples to follow later in the book. The point is, ease yourself into any new changes: don't drink half a bottle of tequila if it's your first time trying alcohol.
5. **Repeat steps one through four.** If you liked your first step in a particular direction. Research more, and keep discussing with friends and loved ones. Then, sample again.

This doesn't mean you should never seek out new adventures, and the vast majority of people drink caffeine and show off their thighs without peril. Beware, though, leaving the church puts you in a complicated mental space. For many, it's a scary time filled with angry words from family and the loss of what were once precious truths. Anyone going through significant change and potential heartache will not be in the best space to make potentially life-altering decisions.

This can be a recipe for disaster for someone looking to have sex for the first time. For example, anyone with access to a dating app could conceivably find someone to have sex with them within a few days. Just because you *can* do something doesn't mean you *should* do something.

Do you know about protection? Birth control? STD and STI prevention? How to ensure consent? How to communicate effectively? How to provide pleasure for both parties? If you can't confidently answer these questions, refer to the list of steps above.

These cases illustrate a general principle of leaving the church and seeking new experiences—don't move so quickly that you make mistakes you'll regret. You have the entirety of the rest of your life. Give yourself space to clear your head. Then, when it is time to try something new, you can experience it fully.

MIND YOUR MENTAL HEALTH

As I shared in the first few chapters, when I left the church, I was in the middle of a severe bout of depression. I was having a hard time concentrating and sleeping. Instead of going out for a walk or talking with friends, I wanted to lay in bed. Whenever I was driving alone, I would turn on some Enya and cry.

After I filled my first antidepressant prescription, I looked down at the one-month supply of tiny white pills and thought—*what a shockingly optimistic number of pills*. I didn't expect to use all 30 pills because I didn't expect to make it 30 more days. As you pause during this chapter and in your life, take stock of your current mental state.

A faith crisis can lead to a mental health crisis. If your family, spouse, and friends are upset with you, you may feel more isolated than ever before. This makes it even harder to ask for help. When I believed in God, I could pray when I was sad or upset. After losing my faith, I didn't have a God to chat with anymore. So many supports were removed. Some may face homelessness due to a faith transition in the most severe cases.

There's a chance you feel completely fine and unaffected by the change. Be careful jumping to this conclusion. You've left behind your religion and possibly lost some friends and family. Do not blow off this moment in an attempt to quickly move on. The pain stays with you till you deal with it. We avoid discomfort to keep ourselves safe in the short term, but this does more damage in the long term. You cannot shove away all your negative feelings and emotions forever—they'll bubble back up at some point.

Take the mental health questionnaire on the following pages and then count up your score. Depending on your results, make a plan to address what you're experiencing. See a counselor or primary care provider if your symptoms are more severe. Many universities offer free counseling. In addition, community centers, hospitals, and schools may provide free or low-cost counseling.

If seeing a provider is not possible for you, try to address your symptoms independently. Write a list of activities you can easily do to increase your well-being. Something as simple as walking can boost your serotonin and increase energy levels.

After making your list, write a schedule to guarantee you do at least one activity per day. It may sound cheesy, but actively protecting and healing your mental health is supremely important during this incredibly tumultuous period of life.

DEPRESSION QUESTIONNAIRE

Over the last ***two weeks****, how often have you been bothered by any of the following problems?* *Circle a score for each*	Not at all	Several days	More than half the days	Nearly every day
Little interest or pleasure in doing things	0	1	2	3
Feeling down, depressed, or hopeless	0	1	2	3
Trouble falling asleep, staying asleep, or sleeping too much	0	1	2	3
Feeling tired or having little energy	0	1	2	3
Poor appetite or overeating	0	1	2	3
Feeling bad about yourself—that you are a failure or you have let yourself or your family down	0	1	2	3
Trouble concentrating on things—like reading or watching television	0	1	2	3
Moving or speaking so slowly that others could have noticed or the opposite—being so fidgety or restless that you have been moving around more than usual	0	1	2	3
Thoughts that you would be better off dead or hurting yourself in some way	0	1	2	3

SCORING INTERPRETATION

Score	Interpretation
0-4	**None to minimal depression** Continue monitoring and doing things that give you a sense of well-being.
5-9	**Mild depression** Continue monitoring and seek out activities that give you a sense of well-being. Make a plan to incorporate those activities into your day-to-day life.
10-14	**Moderate depression** Actively monitor how you are feeling from day to day. Moderate depression will impact your well-being. Incorporate activities to support your mental health every day. Consider scheduling an appointment with a counselor or with your primary care doctor; they will help you find solutions.
15-19	**Moderately severe depression** Actively monitor how you are feeling from day to day. Moderately severe depression is impacting your well-being. Incorporate activities to support your mental health every day. It is recommended that you schedule an appointment with a counselor or with your primary care doctor; they will help you find solutions.
20-27	**Severe depression** Actively monitor how you are feeling from day to day. Severe depression is greatly impacting your well-being. Incorporate activities to support your mental health every morning and evening. It is strongly recommended that you schedule an appointment with a counselor or with your primary care doctor; they will help you find solutions. There is relief available.

If you answered anything besides 0 on question #9: You answered that you have been having thoughts that you would be better off dead or hurting yourself. Please reach out for help. Contact someone you trust about your thoughts and feelings. If you are thinking about suicide, call the National Suicide Prevention Lifeline at 1-800-273-8255 at any time, day or night, to speak with a trained counselor. It's free and confidential.

ANYWHERE YOU WANT

In a 2016 conference session, M. Russell Ballard asked members struggling with their faith: "Where will you go?"

The talk asserts there is no place to find truth and happiness outside the Mormon doctrine. His talk is a warning to those tempted to leave. The question reminds me of what a parent might say when a little child threatens to run away.

Dr. Seuss addressed the same topic in one of my favorite children's books. While Ballard hopes to cast fear into the hearts of those listening to his talk, Seuss does the opposite. While Ballard asks, "Where will you go?" Dr. Seuss wrote, "Oh, the Places You'll Go!"

The "real world" is not a terrifying hellscape of unhappiness. Instead, it's full of endless possibilities. And while the character in "Oh, the Places You'll Go!" has to climb mountains and face adversity, it makes him better. It helps him grow. Stepping outside the church is intimidating but worth it in exchange for growth and discovery. As Dr. Seuss wrote:

> You have brains in your head.
> You have feet in your shoes.
> You can steer yourself
> Any direction you choose.
> You're on your own. And you know what you know.
> And YOU are the guy who'll decide where to go.

Do not take M. Russell Ballard's question as a warning; take it as a challenge. Where will you go? Oh, the places you'll go! Who will you be? What can you accomplish outside the limiting beliefs and narratives the church perpetuates? Where will you travel? Who will you meet along the way? What books will you read? What ideas will you discover? Who will you become?

As I reflect on who I was as a church member, I see a life marked by a constant desire to be the best Mormon I could be. I discarded so many parts of myself. So many dreams and desires vanished in the face of Mormonism.

Instead of pursuing a career in writing, I chose to be a teacher because I blindly followed revelation given in a blessing. Instead of traveling and joining the Peace Corps, I decided to serve a mission. I ended some close friendships because they didn't fit the Mormon mold—even though I gravitated toward these fascinating people. I changed my clothes, how I spoke, and what I did with my time. This was all to align myself as closely as possible with the Mormon ideal.

When I finally stepped away, I realized I had no idea who I was or what I wanted. I spent so long pushing down any thought, idea, or desire that fell outside of Mormonism. I couldn't fully hear my voice anymore. There was more space for God in my brain than for my own identity.

Once I reframed leaving in my mind—to take my experience from "Where will you go?" to "Oh the places you'll go," everything changed. After two decades of rejecting my desires and identity, I could finally embrace myself without guilt or revulsion. I am ready to answer Ballard's threatening question, "Where will you go?"

So, to Elder Ballard and anyone with the same question: **I'll go wherever I want to go.**

REFLECT AND WRITE

- Is there an experience you've never tried due to your religious beliefs? What is it? What emotions do you feel as you consider making this choice?
- You will have extra time on your hands now you're not spending Sundays at church. No more church callings. No more cleaning the building. What are some things you want to do with this extra time? Napping, exercising, time with family, etc.
- What do you think happens after you die? What do you hope happens? How might these new beliefs change how you move through life?
- The church advises against tattoos and piercings. You've probably only dressed in a very modest, conservative way in the past. Are there any changes you want to make now that you're out of the church? How do you feel about potential changes?
- As you exit the church, are there any assumptions about sex and sexuality you feel ready to challenge? What aspects of sex and sexuality do you want to explore?
- The Word of Wisdom prohibits a laundry list of substances, from coffee to drugs and alcohol. What choices
- Now that tithing is a thing of the past, you'll have a bigger chunk of change in your account each month. What do you want to do with the money? Investing, donating elsewhere, a car payment, etc.

REMOVING YOUR NAME

As we pause in this chapter, addressing a common Exmormon question seems appropriate. I took my name off the church rosters in 2019. It used to be a fairly difficult and stressful process involving writing a letter and speaking with your bishop or stake president. With QuitMormon.com, removing your name can be completed online. This website connects you with lawyers who help remove your name, and they do it for free.

To remove your name, you need your full name, birth date, address, membership number (this is not required if you don't have it), and email address. You will also need to notarize your resignation documentation, which can be completed at a post office or UPS. A notary costs between ten to twenty dollars.

It took a month or so before I heard back from the church: my name was officially removed. Once you are an adult, your parents will usually not know you removed your name. My mom didn't find out for several years until I broke the news. They may find out if you are still in their ward or stake, but as long as your records are separated from theirs, they will have no way of knowing. If it is critical your family never discovers you've left the church, it is best to be safe and keep your name on church records.

I removed my name because I no longer wanted it associated with the church. My name belongs to me, not to the church. The church is very outspoken about its colossal membership, and I didn't want to give them the privilege of adding my name to their numbers. While I recognize one individual doesn't make a big difference to the church, it means a lot to me.

Some people keep their names on because they are still struggling in the messy middle of belief and they aren't ready to sever ties yet. Some people hope to get excommunicated, and they keep their names on the records (this is how Jackson wants to go). Others feel that even though they no longer believe in the church's truth claims, they are culturally Mormon. They maintain their membership for personal reasons.

You do not have to remove your name to leave the church. It was a moment of great significance when I took my name off the records. There was a sense of finality about it. Other people don't care at all about this gesture. If you want to remove your name, know it is very straightforward, and it's doubtful anyone close to you will be able to find out. Removing your name is a very personal choice, so follow your feelings.

CHOOSE YOUR OWN ADVENTURE

Pause here and return to Chapter Two. Find the "Social and Religious Spectrum" table on page 44. Consider your original placement and decide if you need to update your dot or are still in the same headspace. If you change your position, write the current date next to your second dot to plot your movement over time. Add the date, and write an explanation, if you choose, off to the side.

Chapters one through four focus on the initial faith crisis and the phases that follow immediately after you begin to question the church. If you've finished these first four chapters, I assume you've made and shared your decision. You have started to consider what life outside the church will look like for you. The rest of this book is a compilation of the significant areas of life to explore outside the church.

There are many practical decisions to consider. If you want to try coffee, walking into a Starbucks and reading the menu is intimidating. I still can't remember the difference between a venti and a grande straight. What's the difference between a latte, an americano, and drip coffee? Do you want oat milk? One or two shots of espresso? Is it pronounced EX-presso or ES-presso? (It's the latter.)

Going into a bar can be daunting, and ordering a drink is even more unnerving. Beer or wine? What about a cocktail? Do you prefer tequila or whiskey? How much can you drink before you get drunk? When can you safely drive home? How much should you tip your bartender?

When you grow up outside of the church, you learn a lot of this from your parents and friends. When you hear your parents order coffee, you pick up the jargon and begin to make assumptions about what you will enjoy.

However, the language, social expectations, and newness keep some people from ever trying new experiences outside the church. This goes for Word of Wisdom-type experiences but also pertains to many other aspects of life. You may feel ready to explore your sexuality past the heteronormative expectations of the church. Have you changed your political leanings? Do you have sexist or racist assumptions to confront and challenge?

Feel free to choose your own adventure for the remainder of this book. You could continue to read through each chapter page by page, or you can flip to whatever chapters or sections are the most relevant to you now. When I first left, I was excited to try out drinking. I was not ready to investigate anything to do with sexuality.

You may not be emotionally ready to scrutinize all the aspects of your identity outside the church. That is completely normal and probably healthy, too. Change is scary. Your brain wants you to stay sane, and familiarity is safety. At the same time, change is also invigorating and exciting. Step carefully and purposefully. Make sure you are in an emotionally good place before making any major decisions. If you want to skip ahead to read about a particular subject, review the following index. Otherwise, keep reading.

SIX
REBELLION
Break All the Little Rules

Freedom lies in being bold.

—Robert Frost

When I turned eight, I fell into a strange, childish suicidality. It sounds odd, but it's not uncommon for tiny members of the church. My desire to die before my eighth birthday wasn't linked to any tangibly dark portions of my life—only to my fear of sin. I remember constant conversations about "the age of accountability." Persistent reminders: *Right now, you are perfect. Once you are eight, sin will stain you.*

This transition was drilled home innumerable ways through primary lessons, family conversations, and even song. When I made a mistake, the words to "When I Am Baptized" echoed in my mind, "I want my life to be as clean as earth right after rain."

Repentance seemed thin and cheap compared to the perfection I was told I embodied as a pure seven-year-old. I didn't want to *need* repentance. I didn't want to be able to sin at all. By my childlike logic, it seemed better to die at seven than to risk damnation at eight.

As I sat in the car after my baptism, I stared at my reflection in the dusty driver's side mirror. I considered my countenance, a word often used in my family. I looked the same as yesterday but knew I had foundationally changed at the core. I would never be pure again. It was the age of accountability, and the immaculately sterling years of my childhood were in the past.

This overwhelming religious guilt lingered throughout my years in the church. Doctrinally, taking the sacrament and repentance should be as good as baptism, but it never felt that way. When I made a sinful choice, I would sit in my room and cry and cry. Strange to me now that my "sinful choices" were brief, unkind words or making a Myspace page without permission. There was no drug use, stealing, underage drinking, or premarital sex in my squeaky-clean life. I never even considered participating in any risky behaviors typical of teenage years.

Still, the slightest hint of transgression threw me into a tear-stained anguish. Lessons on the atonement detailed how I inflicted blinding pain on Jesus Christ every time I sinned. When I watched those gratuitously violent films recounting the crucifixion, my wickedness was the whip splitting open Christ's flesh. My guilt was more intense than any death row inmate.

Something changed after I stood up and left Relief Society for the last time. I passed through a semipermeable membrane, sliding away from primary lessons on sin and the doctrine of repentance. This Mormon moral framework of R-rated movies, alcohol, and tank tops melted off me. Sin was a construct, not an undeniable truth. And when I sipped my first bit of coffee in a Starbucks, I wanted to laugh. Drinking coffee did not change my DNA—it did not morph me into some nasty, warty demon.

I was still me. And as I began living life outside of Mormonism, the smoke and mirrors of it all became foolish and absurd. What I once considered massively "immoral" choices became fun weekends and morning routines. As soon as I stripped all the guilt and sin away from my life, I began to walk on happy clouds. Nothing could hurt me—swearing, drinking, and pornography—none of it had any level of power over me.

Instead of outsourcing my identity and worth to Mormonism and Jesus, I finally held it within. All the religious messaging from my childhood and adolescence is what actually damaged me. I was wounded by the shame taught in Young Women's lessons. My everyday choices did not make me evil.

Sometimes, I still walk back over the same well-worn paths from my time in the church. Mental trails of guilt and shame are so familiar that it's hard to ignore them completely. My choices are unanchored from constant moral negotiation. I no longer picture Jesus getting whipped when I think of some unkind thing in passing.

As you enter into this new time of life, embrace moral complexity. For so long, the monochromatic thinking of the church has thrown every choice into black and white—and every shade of white into "good, better, and best." Finally, after all this time, you can do what *you* want and what *you* think is best. Divorce your mind from *what would Jesus do* and only consider the wants and needs of those you love, and of yourself.

As you read this chapter, read it as a list of suggestions, not rules. I'm not writing scripture here. And while I found a lot of excitement in experimentation after leaving the church, it doesn't mean you will. After losing your testimony, you may still be primarily interested in a simple existence. I wanted to move to New York and get tattoos. You may wish to remain in Utah and live a traditional life.

Both choices are valid. A life somewhere in the middle is valuable, too. I have tattoos, and I enjoy wine. I'm also a stay-at-home mom with two kids. Redefining myself after Mormonism meant keeping the pieces from my previous existence that still mattered to me. You can chart this course for yourself. You can now live whatever version of life you want, be it run-of-the-mill or wild and unrestrained.

Discover who hides under guilt, sin, and doctrinal heaviness. Choose to live with courage. Writing this book is my wild and fierce choice—a way to reclaim my story. What blazing, meteoric existence will you live now that your life is your own?

One of my favorite photos documenting my exit from the church is of me gleefully holding a cup of coffee in Salt Lake. I felt mischievous—casually committing a crime in plain sight. When I visit Utah from time to time, I enjoy watching the people's faces as they try to place me. So much of me seems Mormon, but the nose ring and tattoos defy an LDS categorization. The confusion grows when I casually mention serving a mission, and active members typically look at me with a mix of judgment and pity. Their crestfallen expression says, "How could one with so much truth fall away?"

As I walked through a church building a year after I left, someone in a suit approached me and said hello. He referred to me as "Sister" and began a conversation with a level of Mormon familiarity. My soul squirmed. Though I was only in the building for a wedding, my clothing and the way I presented myself immediately transformed me back into Sister Grenfell. It was like nothing had changed, and in that tiny space of time, my identity was still trapped in the claws of the church.

Standing in front of the mirror that night, I searched my face and body for the remaining signs of Mormon Me. Mormons love to talk about the "light in the eyes" of faithful followers of Christ. Despite all my drinking and covenant-breaking, the man in the church saw my blonde hair, modest dress, and cheesy smile and pegged me for a Mormon, through and through. My closet was still full of garment-approved clothing. My hair and makeup matched the stereotypical Utah-girl style. There's no way I would even raise an eyebrow at the BYU testing center.

I was surprised by how much it bothered me to be mistaken for a Mormon. And while it may not fundamentally matter what I look like to others, I still felt the need to reclaim my image and all of the pieces inside me. My body finally belonged to me again, but all my years of careful styling ensured I still appeared very Mormon.

Maybe you should not get a tattoo or piercing simply so you don't "look Mormon" anymore. That is not what I'm suggesting here. Rather, being a member of the church often means you look a certain way.

As a man, this means always cutting your hair to match a particular style, shaving, looking clean-cut, and probably wearing too much BYU gear (or, at the very least, too many pairs of basketball shorts). For a woman, it means always covering your shoulders and knees, wearing the right amount of makeup, only wearing one pair of earrings, avoiding coloring your hair, and shunning tight or revealing clothing.

These laundry lists of what Mormons should look like are extremely limiting—the church compels members to look like housewives and businessmen from the fifties. When stopped by the man in the church building, I realized there was another mountain to conquer: my image.

TATTOOS

Most of the Exmormons I meet would like to get a tattoo at some point, and even the church has loosened up on the topic. Tattoo choices are intimate and permanent—research many different designs and artists to find your perfect fit. My tattoos are for my family: one for Jackson and one tattoo for each son. I figure if your tattoos represent the most important people and things in your life—how wicked can they really be?

Mormons are right about one thing: tattoos last a lifetime and are painful to remove. But rather than avoiding them altogether, make your choice carefully. Or get something silly and fun. Choose what moves you! Don't be thrifty when choosing a shop or an artist—you get what you pay for. You can get a fake tattoo printed if you're unsure about a specific design. Experiment with the design and placement before you get the real thing. Despite common depictions in the media, tattoos do not hurt too terribly. To me, it feels like a minor burn, and the feeling goes away pretty quickly. Of course, the level of intensity varies with your pain tolerance and the specifics of your chosen tattoo.

Placement is essential for those hoping to hide tattoos from judgemental friends, family, or employers. Anywhere a bathing suit covers is a good bet. My first tattoo was the letter "J" on my wrist—solidly in the open for all to see. Tattoos are deeply personal; choose a placement and design for yourself, not out of fear of judgment.

I got my first tattoo when I was twenty-six, and I didn't share the decision with anyone except for Jackson. My family saw it for the first time when I showed up for Christmas, and though it was certainly noticed, silence was the chosen form of acknowledgment. If you do plan on telling your family beforehand, be prepared for parents and most members to try to dissuade you. There may be less drama if you simply go for it, and then show it off at the next family function. Discouragement doesn't work after the fact when it comes to tattoos.

PIERCINGS

My nose ring is my favorite billboard for the new me. Nothing says heathen like a facial piercing. As Gordon B. Hinkley cautioned in 2000, "Likewise the piercing of the body for multiple rings in the ears, in the nose, even in the tongue. Can they possibly think that is beautiful? It is a passing fancy, but its effects can be permanent."

This talk resulted in a sudden piercing obsession, and a single set of earrings became synonymous with your love for Jesus Christ. I recall one especially tearful testimony from a woman who shared the story of removing her second pair of earrings after she listened to the talk.

Mormons are funny that way—loving Christ is characterized as avoiding R-rated movies, praying to find your car keys, and avoiding too many piercings. Rather than giving talks from the pulpit about working at soup kitchens and sharing your home with refugees, Mormons are convinced the most trivial, banal activities and rule-following are proof of Christlike love. An accurate marker of a faithful Mormon woman has nothing to do with Jesus and everything to do with how many earrings she wears.

What a wonderful new world Exmormons enter, where our bodies are our own. Who cares if anyone but you thinks your piercing is beautiful or badass? If you like it, you do it. All the rest, God included, can go to hell.

On the more practical side of advice, similar to tattoos, research shops and read reviews carefully. Ask friends for shop recommendations. Avoid piercing guns, which are often used in shopping mall settings. Don't let a friend pierce your ears at 2 a.m. Find a professional shop. You can get fake piercing rings or magnetic studs if you want to try on a piercing to see how it suits you.

A piercer will suggest specific placement once you decide on the general area and will use a marker so you can give it final approval before you get pierced. Piercings hurt more than tattoos, in my opinion. It's a pretty quick, sharp pain, and then it's over.

And nothing hurts like the psychological pain of "donating" your income to build a shopping mall, so there's that, too.

CLOTHING AND PERSONAL STYLE

Remember the 10% of your income that you used to hand over to the church? Save that money and spend it on your new wardrobe. If you've worn garments for a year or more, you probably only own garment-approved clothing. After leaving, I kept wearing the same clothes I wore at BYU. I was nervous to wear tank tops and shorts, and I craved the familiarity of my "modest" clothes, even though I wasn't wearing garments underneath anymore.

Changing up a wardrobe or personal look can be intimidating for anyone. However, this becomes even more difficult when you've internalized supreme levels of body shaming throughout your life. The first few times I attempted to wear a tank top out and about, I changed clothing at the last minute. If you live with your parents or if your spouse is still a member, you may get pushback and judgment for wearing "revealing" clothing like shorts or crop tops.

Maybe you feel wary of your shoulders, and you anticipate judgment for wearing clothing you would have avoided in the past. Be patient with yourself, but don't stick your head in the sand. Modest is not hottest—you are hottest when you love your body and are confident in your skin. You're leaving the church, and even baby steps are brave. Your body is not evil. Those who sexualize bodies for merely existing are evil. Your body is a beautiful, powerful force propelling you through the experience of life. Some nice jean shorts can be your gateway drug to an eventual string bikini on the beach.

Shop around online or make a Pinterest board with styles you like. Pinterest has great ideas for women *and* men. Go shopping with a non-judgemental friend and buy a few items you wouldn't have worn in the past. First, wear them alone around the house and get comfortable. Then, wear your new clothes to an event or place where you feel at ease.

Men in the church have fewer clothing restrictions, but this doesn't mean you won't have inhibitions. There is a very particular way a good Mormon man should look. Elders collect strange and unique ties in an effort to maintain some level of individuality. Mormon men have very few ways to assert identity.

For men, reclaiming your look may mean growing a beard or growing your hair long. You may get a few tattoos and buy your first Speedo. Get a piercing or wear shirts with offensive bands like *The Sex Pistols*. Dress in pink. Add crazy color and design. Choose an influential figure you admire, study how they carry themselves, and define their image.

You may find that tank tops are outrageously comfortable. Several Exmormon men have expressed a newfound love of shorts cut higher above the knee. In the broader culture, men wear clothing that easily pairs with garments, so you may want to keep your clothes the same. My friend, Levi, shared his journey to self-acceptance as he left the church. His story is below.

LEVI'S STORY

> The church places far fewer restrictions on men, but we're still taught that we represent the Savior. This comes with a strict style guide. If your Sunday shirt isn't white, you can't bless the sacrament. Leaders can't wear bowties. No earrings. No tattoos.

"Avoid the appearance of evil." A hot chocolate in a Starbucks cup is as bad as a coffee. This constant focus on appearance and what others think can fuck anyone up.

I grew up in Utah, where most Mormon boys have straight blonde hair, a smooth white face, and slender builds ideal for running. I have dark, curly hair, a face speckled with freckles, and a naturally stocky body—gifts from my dad's Scottish ancestors and my mom's Polynesian roots.

In elementary school, I remember looking at my friends' skinny ankles. Their socks stretched around their Achilles tendons, leaving gaps on either side. They looked spry and agile. My ankles filled my socks like a cupcake in its liner. Their calves were slender; mine were thick and beefy. I wondered if more girls would like me if I looked like the other boys. I felt ashamed of my body and wanted to cover my legs.

From ages eleven to twenty-seven, I didn't wear shorts. I avoided pool parties. Our apartment complex had a very nice community pool during my senior year of high school. I never used it.

Reminders of my differences weren't always from inside my head. As a seventeen-year-old priest, the bishop emphasized my distinctive curly hair by comparing me to animals in front of the other boys. Alpaca. Llama. Poodle. Sheep. I later found out one of the other boys straightened his hair every morning.

Ten years later, I left the church. I no longer believed I had to represent the Son of God or look like the typical example of a good Mormon boy. I felt more empowered to love myself for my differences.

At twenty-eight years old (and with much love and encouragement from my wife), I felt more secure than ever and bought my first pair of shorts as an adult. I chose a pair of bright red, extra-short Adidas. It was my way of plunging into the deep end.

Now, I believe my wife when she says she loves my curly hair, thick legs, and broad build. People ask what my leg workout is. Girls use brow pens to draw faux freckles. K-pop stars get perms to have curly hair. So many of my "differences" are normal or desired when you look outside of the church.

I don't need to look or dress like one of the 90-year-old apostles or their most dedicated followers to be a good person. I don't need to have runner's legs to be strong or straight hair to be handsome. I've stopped wondering if Moroni's command to "be perfect" means I should look more like someone else. I only need to be enough for myself—and I am.

UNDERWEAR

While you're planning and purchasing your new wardrobe, grab some sexy underwear. Garments are impossibly frumpy, and even if you were never endowed, chances are you have some pretty conservative underclothing. For women, Victoria's Secret is an obvious brick-and-mortar choice, and there are tons of options online. For men, Calvin Klein is a favorite. For couples, MeUndies is an online shop where you and your partner can buy matching sets.

Buy yourself a thong, something with tons of lace, and something black. Men can buy thongs too, or buy some nice silky boxers—it's up to you. I'm sure a partner will love your choices, but you should buy some fun underwear even if you're single. Gift it to yourself and wear it around the house or under your everyday clothes.

Wearing garments is a very intimate part of membership in the church. Very little in life is more private than your underwear. When I left the church, wearing my garments became more dreadful by the day. It felt fundamentally wrong to continue to wear garments; they made my skin crawl.

The choice to stop wearing garments is more tangible and physical than the choice to stop praying or stop reading your scriptures. It's not a slow taper. I had to get in my car, drive to a store, and buy new underwear. I wore garments for more than three years, so I didn't have any other underwear lying around.

If you're ready to buy underwear, do it sooner rather than later. It's liberating. Some people leave the church at twenty-one and some at sixty-one. You're never too old to read this book or to stop believing. Maybe you've worn garments for thirty-plus years. When you buy new underwear without symbols, you'll probably feel an avalanche of emotion. I congratulate you for courageously living in a new reality.

This will leave you with an enormous pile of garments and all your temple clothing. You may keep your temple clothes in the closet as a memory. You can also burn them or trash them. Some people use them as a Halloween costume, while others keep them in case they return to the church someday. Others save their garments to wear around family members who they aren't "out" to yet. I threw mine away. It felt amazing. My body is mine again. I almost forgot how I looked naked.

REFLECT AND WRITE

The rest of this chapter is dedicated to other rules and cultural taboos permeating Mormon belief. Consider the following questions, and reflect on your feelings as you continue to read. Note the feelings bubbling up inside you at the prospect of swearing, gambling, or throwing away your garments. What does this reveal about you and your faith transition?

- ✦ How has the concept of sin influenced your decisions and actions in life?
- ✦ If you were to get a tattoo, piercing, or change your image in some way, what would it symbolize for you? How could this impact your self-image and confidence?
- ✦ What aspects of your identity have evolved since leaving the church? How has leaving Mormonism impacted your self-acceptance and self-esteem?
- ✦ What changes do you want to make as you redefine your image and appearance?

TITHING

I always paid tithing without thinking. My Mormon mind felt righteous glee as 10% of my income slipped from my bank account. When I worked at Dairy Queen in high school, hundreds of dollars of cash touched my hands throughout an eight-hour shift. Though my drawer was stuffed with money, I never considered putting a quarter of it in my pocket. And so it was with tithing.

The money wasn't mine; it was the Lord's. My mom always taught us to pay on our gross earnings instead of the net. "Pay the

Lord before you pay the government," was her explanation. This made perfect sense to me.

Only after I left and looked back at tithing statements did I realize how much money I had given to the church. Imagine stacking all the money you've funneled to the church over your life. Include the unpaid service in callings, paying for the "privilege" to go on a mission, fast offering, and, of course, the 10% tithe. That stack of cash would reach the moon and back.

When you leave the church, you get a pay increase of 10%. As you begin to enjoy your pay raise, plan what you want to do with it. You could pay off your car or house more quickly, but I suggest holding off on the "boring" expenses for a few pay cycles. Use the money for fun.

Go on a road trip, fly to Europe, pay for your new non-Mormon wardrobe, or take up a hobby you always felt was too expensive. It's time to tithe that money to yourself. That money is still sacred, but instead of sending it to a multi-billion dollar corporation, you can use it to improve your life. Pay for therapy and get that Master's Degree you always wanted but couldn't afford. Use the money to support a family member.

You can also consider investing your would-be tithing money. As a Mormon woman, I was rarely exposed to any measure of financial literacy. I knew saving money was important, but learning to be thrifty is different from learning to invest in the stock market. Men are significantly more likely to take finance classes and learn how to make and invest money. These lessons are rarely instilled in women in the church.

If you don't know the difference between stocks and bonds, don't know what a 401k is, and don't know what the term "return on investment" means, it is time to get financially literate. Money is power. If your spouse is exclusively responsible for your finances, please let that era pass.

When you understand money, you know how to provide for yourself and your loved ones. Read books about the stock market, real estate investing, and retirement accounts. Listen to finance podcasts. Begin to track your net worth. Grow an emergency fund. Yes, it may be boring, but these are the steps you need to take to harness this power for yourself. You risk being taken advantage of if you don't understand your financial situation.

While reflecting on how to use your tithing money, don't throw away the Mormon urge to donate toward a worthy cause. While you tithe your 10% back to yourself, you can also set some money aside to give to charities and causes. As a member, I loved the feeling of donating to people in need. Unfortunately, this was really only a feeling since most tithing money goes straight into an investment account rather than to real charity work.

Research charities doing meaningful work and donate to them. An organization like Giving What We Can is an organization where members pledge to give at least 10% of their income to charity. They emphasize a goal to end world hunger. Before donating, always do your homework on the particular organization. Many charitable organizations make great promises but don't consistently deliver due to corruption or bureaucratic bloat. Find an organization you believe in and donate to the community and the world.

SECOND SATURDAYS

As an adult, you likely spent your weeks working Monday through Friday, enjoying the day off on Saturday, and going to church on Sunday. Though the church has shifted from a three-hour schedule to a two-hour schedule, Sundays are still more or less dedicated to the Lord. My family was not allowed to watch TV on Sundays (except for The Prince of Egypt or Johnny Lingo). My mom preferred we remain in uncomfortable church clothes for the entire day. Visiting teachers and home teachers made visits; sometimes, it was Fast Sunday, and I was starving out of my mind.

Saturday remained the one pure day—the only day reserved to do whatever you wanted. Though growing up, my family would still sing the song, "Saturday is a special day, it's the day you get ready for Sunday." The church attempts to steal Saturday by mandating church building cleanups and extensive preparations for Sunday. My obsession with Saturday grew when I started teaching 9th grade. I was burned out from giving so much of myself to work and to church. There was never much left in the bucket for me to scrape out.

As I struggled with leaving the church, I read a quote by Henry David Thoreau, "Most men lead lives of quiet desperation and go to the grave with the song still in them." I knew if I continued in the church—if I kept my head down and carried on with the life I already knew—I would die with a massive symphony unplayed inside me. When I use Sunday to paint, run, or write, I sing my own song.

Leaving the church is more than missing a two-hour block; it's getting the entire day back. Second Saturday is one of the most impactful and immediate perks of leaving the church. Trade your boring chapel for a day spent in nature. Exchange the unprepared Sunday school lesson for a tipsy Sunday brunch.

I do encourage a throughline in the approach to tithing and second Saturdays. While the church is not true, it does encourage you to approach each new week with purpose. Your tithing money was sacred and consecrated, and your Sunday worship was too. As mentioned in the last section, keeping a portion of your life and your money holy is a good practice. I've loved continuing this out of the church—sans God.

Use your second Saturday as a time devoted to your best self. This could mean exercising, volunteering, learning something new, catching up with an old friend, or writing in a journal. It may mean reading a new book, napping, or learning a new recipe. Just as you can use your tithing to invest back into yourself, your life, and your community, do the same with your newfound extra day of the week.

FILM, MUSIC, AND OTHER MEDIA

When I was a kid sleeping over at a friend's house, I caught a glance of a movie my friend's parents were watching. Austin Powers and his cheeky smile flashed from the screen; he giggled while blonde girls in pink lingerie seduced him. I was convinced I had watched porn. The guilt was overwhelming, but I was worried that if I told my parents, I wouldn't be able to see my friend anymore.

Fifteen years later, Jackson and I watched *Austin Powers: International Man of Mystery*. Silly as it may be, the movie haunted me for so long. It felt like a mountain to conquer on my way out of the church—to laugh at a silly movie and prove watching it didn't make me immoral. What had once felt like the most gratuitous and wicked porn unraveled into dumb jokes and blondes shooting bullets from their bras.

When the movie was finished, we laughed and talked and then went to bed. I didn't get hit by a bus the next day or choke on my breakfast on the way to work. Satan didn't push into my soul and force me to kill puppies with my bare hands. I felt tremendous relief—the film had no power over me. It was a dumb, silly, funny movie. This thing I had believed was a tool of the devil, built to lead me away from Christ, was a little bit of frivolous nothingness.

In the years after I left, I consumed all the media I had ever been told was immoral. I watched *The Hangover*, *Superbad*, *The 40-Year-Old Virgin*. I listened to as much Britney Spears as I wanted. My family was not allowed to watch *The Hunchback of Notre Dame* because Esmeralda was "a woman of the night"—so I watched that too. When the song "WAP" by Cardi B and Megan Thee Stallion came out, I read the lyrics and laughed so hard.

Across the course of my childhood and adolescence, I was convinced so much popular media was darkly sinful. I carefully highlighted my *For the Strength of Youth* pamphlet and internalized: "Satan uses such entertainment to deceive you by making what is wrong and evil look normal and exciting. It can mislead you into thinking that everyone is doing things that are wrong."

Leaving the church made me realize how much pop culture I had rejected entirely. There was so much music I wasn't familiar with, so many movies I missed out on, and art I shunned. Friends would reference *Pink Floyd* or David Bowie, and I was utterly lost. I knew nothing about *Queen* or the *Red Hot Chili Peppers*. Discovering a vast new world of art and music was one of my favorite parts of leaving the church. Conquering my internalized guilt for enjoying whatever content I wanted was extraordinarily empowering.

Plan to use some of your second Saturday to do a media deep dive and to watch all the movies your parents said were bad as a kid. *The Godfather, Pretty Woman, The Shawshank Redemption, Schindler's List, Pulp Fiction,* and *The Matrix* are a few of my favorites. There are so many fantastic R-rated movies. Each genre of music contains days' worth of songs to enjoy. These pieces of media are the most influential cultural cornerstones of our time. And some of them are great to watch while high, like *Dumb and Dumber* and *The Big Lebowski*.

SWEARING

Using swear words was like an avalanche for me—total silence, then a thunderous, all-at-once roar. For the first year or so after leaving, I never swore. Theoretically and morally, I was "okay" with swearing. In reality, I still had quite a mental block. "Damn" and "hell" weren't in my vocabulary, and "shit" and "fuck" were entirely out of the question. Even words for anatomy like "penis" and "vagina" were barely muttered when there was an absolute need. Any taboo word got stuck between my teeth and swallowed back down. *Austin Powers* and *The Hunchback of Notre Dame* were my religious boogiemen, and swearing was similarly spooky.

On a camping trip around the new year, I shared my resolution to start swearing more. We spent the night practicing. At first, I said each word like I might hold a bird, anxiously and gently, like it might die if I grip it the wrong way. Then, after running a few drills, I began to get the hang of it. "Jesus *FUCKING* Christ, these smores are good," I shouted into the void.

Saying these words out loud broke a magic spell. I pulled back the curtain of forbidden and unspeakable taboos to reveal a bumbling man who only had power because I gave it to him to begin with. Saying "fuck" doesn't make me an immoral person. Using "Jesus Christ!" as an exclamation will not turn me into a smelly rotten pumpkin. Swearing is incredibly fun.

As Mark Twain said, "Under certain circumstances, profanity provides a relief denied even to prayer." Letting all the swears loose is the linguistic parallel to cathartically breaking an entire cabinet's worth of dishes. Swearing is even more fun when you're willing to get creative. Some colorful favorites in my repertoire include, "Eat a bag of dicks!" and "Jesus, Mary, and Joseph!" and, of course, "Fuck you, you fucking piece of shit!"

Why stop at words when you can also swear with your hands? The middle finger is as versatile as the day is long. To say "fuck you" in sign language, move your palm to face your chest, right under your chin. Then, extend your hand outward, keeping your hand high, almost flicking your chin with the top of your hand. There are so many ways to offend!

If you want to swear, but don't know where to start, begin by saying the simplest words. I call them "Bible swears." Sing along to your favorite vulgar songs. Damn, hell and ass are "beginner-level" swears. "Butt" was a bad word in my home growing up, so even forcing myself to say that was a little intimidating.

Whisper them in the bathroom to yourself in the mirror or use them in a conversation with a nonmember friend. After a few Bible swears, move on to the middle-of-the-road "bitch" and "shit."

Once you round those bases, prepare for your final home run by screaming. "You fucking cunt!"—preferably out the window during the calmest time of day in your neighborhood. If you can do this, you've officially earned the title *Master of Curses*.

GAMBLING

As a kid, I recall my nonmember grandparents leaning against a dusty gas station counter, chatting with the cashier. Obliviously staring at the candy section, I was startled when my grandma asked me to list my favorite numbers. I shared I was partial to zero and three, but my favorite number was twenty-six—my birth date. She then turned and asked my sister for her favorite numbers, and I looked up to see the cashier writing something down as she spoke.

After a moment, my grandparents paid, and the man passed a colorful slip across the counter. My stomach dropped as I read "*Lotto*" printed across the top of the paper. I glanced at my sister, who had seen the slip, too. Our expressions matched. Back at home, we debated whether we should tell our parents. Maybe we should sweep it under the rug. There was that age-old feeling, the same sensation that appeared when I saw Austin Powers dance across the screen. I had "played the lottery," and even though we had done it accidentally and unwillingly, the sin was no less grave.

A few days passed, and guilt seeped into every interaction and every breath. While I felt it was best to keep it a secret, my sister had other plans. She told my parents a week after the initial sinful event. Thus began the onslaught of daily conversations and weekly one-on-one lessons reviewing *For the Strength of Youth* together.

Years later, I found myself in Las Vegas, and newly out of the church. I stood nervously in front of a slot machine. It loomed over me, and I was halfway convinced it would topple over and kill me in an act of cosmic Mormon justice. Placing a few coins in the metal slot, it lit up and sang a little electric song. The rows rotated, arranging carefully into a line of fruits and numbers. A low two-toned "bum bum" announced I hadn't won anything. I waited for the other shoe to drop unceremoniously on my head, but after a few seconds, it was clear there would be no immediate heavenly discipline.

Poker, the lottery, slot machines. Evil, evil, evil. While gambling can be bad for some people, most can enjoy it and put it aside. Ultimately, after my first few moments at the slot machine passed, my apprehension gave way to disinterest.

If you gamble, be smart. Only use money you don't mind losing completely. Don't get drunk while gambling if it may lead to poor choices with money (it probably will). Play with coins and dollar bills, not twenties—and definitely not with a credit card. Remember, the house always wins. Keep it fun; gambling should be enjoyed, not played with intensely high stakes.

It is fun for a night or two, but then it is time to move on. Mormons do have a point when it comes to substances or gambling—these things can completely ruin your life. However, the vast majority of people can drink without becoming alcoholics. Most can gamble without throwing away their entire savings. While being Mormon was all about black and white, becoming Exmormon is embracing many shades of gray.

FRIENDSHIPS

Whether you live in Utah or some faraway place with few members, you're likely to have a specific type of social group as a church member. As a high schooler in Kentucky, I was friends with the nerds. While they weren't members, they didn't drink or have premarital sex, and most were some flavor of Christian.

As members, you are encouraged to "choose friends who share your values so you can strengthen and encourage each other in living high standards." When I left the church, I lived in Utah, and almost everyone I knew was active. I wasn't looking to drop my Mormon friends, but I was searching for new and different experiences. Broadening horizons and personal change is difficult when almost everything about your life remains the same.

When we moved to New York City, I met Stephanie. Her apartment was decorated with strange sculptures, and she casually discussed the merits of an open relationship. She invited us to a party and walked around with a massive bottle of vodka, passing out shots. Her mom, dressed in the most glamorous gown, paraded around the party. The two took shots together and talked for a while, exchanging X-rated jokes riddled with expletives. It was the first time I ever witnessed this type of mother-daughter friendship. Everyone I met connected to Stephanie was an artist, designer, poet, and moral revolutionary.

There was everyone I had ever met, and then there was Stephanie. I had exchanged BYU church friends and parties ending at 8 p.m. for New York creatives loudly arguing about Salvador Dalí's use of masturbation as a parallel to metamorphosis. At times, my brain struggled to wrap itself around this new world. My lifelong Mormon paradigm burst into millions of pieces of confetti, dancing and swaying around me.

As I walked through the streets of New York, I realized Mormonism was the reason I was there. Within months of leaving the church, we moved from Utah. I told myself it was because New York was an exciting city I wanted to explore. But walking around Crown Heights eating pizza and feeling buzzed, I was finally honest with myself. I was wandering but not lost. After a lifetime of service and commitment to a singular religious experience, I needed the strangeness of New York. I ached to live the lives I might have lived had I never been in the church. I still ache.

As you leave the church, look for your version of New York friends. You don't have to move to a strange new city to find friends who are unique and quirky. You can broaden your social circle without leaving your home, but you must go out and find them.

Think about the types of people you want to meet, then figure out where they spend their time. I hoped to find artists and free thinkers, so I looked in coffee shops, record stores, poetry readings, and farmer's markets. You may hope to encounter entrepreneur types, social justice reformers, or modern-day circus performers. Whoever you look for, try and bump into people who will challenge your preconceived Mormon understanding of the world. Talk with them, ask them the wildest questions in your brain, then sit and discuss.

Every small and big town has people who live daringly, people who love wrapping their minds around experimental ideas. Find people who live unapologetically. Look for friends who stretch your thinking and who pursue paths you want to walk down yourself.

While searching for new friends with fresh ideas, don't forget to nurture the friendships you already have and cherish. You likely have Mormon acquaintances who may want nothing to do with you once you've left the church, but you probably also have member friends who earnestly wish to maintain their friendship with you. Finding new friends is a thrill, and old friends are gold. The people who have known you throughout your life provide comfort and familiarity. Old friends ground you through a time when you feel unmoored and adrift.

After I left, some old mission companions and ward members from adolescence seemed quite judgmental. Other friends were as genuine and loving as ever. Some of my most supportive Mormon friends left the church several years after me, and we were both so grateful to have each other throughout the transition. I have loved supporting my friends through their faith crises, and they have loved having help from someone who understands what they are going through.

A new social circle with nonmembers will help with the process of revealing who you are and what you feel after leaving the church. Old friends help you stay connected with your past. Find people who say things that make your mind flip, whir, and soar. Keep friends who love you and support you, regardless of belief. Combine the old with the new, and build your community.

LOUD LAUGHTER

My mom always chastised us for laughing loudly. Someone would make a funny face or say something ridiculous, and all four of us would howl. "Girls," my mom would scold, "It's inappropriate to laugh too loudly. Stop being so light-minded!"

This never failed to confuse me. While I could get behind most of the many rules we had in our home, this one made no sense. I was content never to say "butt" and to keep my eyes tightly shut during prayer. Missing school dances was fine with me, and I never even asked to wear a bikini. But... really? Loud laughter?

Anyone who has received their endowment understands what I'm getting at here. You make different covenants in the temple with God and promise to obey him. The first time I went through the temple, we arrived at the point in the ceremony where they say to "avoid all light-mindedness, loud laughter, evil speaking of the Lord's anointed, the taking of the name of God in vain, and every other unholy and impure practice."

My mom was sitting right next to me during my first endowment session, and it was all I could do to keep from turning and making a face like *that's why you've been lecturing me all these years?* There are countless sins plaguing the earth: child slavery, forced prostitution, starvation, racism, bigotry, murder, and rape. Apparently, of the many evils to address in the Lord's temple, Jesus is seriously concerned with the Saints being too—*checks notes*—silly.

I hope you laugh as you write your Exmormon bucket list and conquer the boogie men from your past. Chuckle while yelling *fuck* and *shit* and *bitch* during a party at 3 a.m. Giggle while watching *Pineapple Express*. Chortle when you lose $1.50 on slots. Cackle on your canoe on second Saturday. Loudly guffaw when you check your bank account and see 10% more than before. Laugh—every new day and new experience—LOUDLY.

There's an obsession with saying the church is True, gambling is a Sin, and drinking is Evil. Mormon doctrine asserts absolute knowledge on nearly every topic. This house of cards collapses when you interact with many people who drink and realize they are neither bad people nor addicts. The same goes for loud laughter, tattoos, coffee, and most of the other concepts in this book. Train yourself to stop assigning definitive value to yourself, experiences, and ways of living.

Of course, if you want, try coffee and alcohol when you leave the church—and buy that tank top you always wanted to wear—but search more deeply for where Mormonism stays rooted in you. Dig and unearth yourself beneath the layers of Mormon traditionalism. Keep the pieces you value and cherish. Throw away the guilt, shame, and judgment.

Most of all, do everything with intention. Move forward carefully and with consideration. Look inward for direction in your life. Stop the urge to think about what a good Mormon would do. Ignore the judgment you might face if you post on social media. Disregard what your mom might think. Don't swear because I wrote you should. Don't drink solely because you saw a post on r/Exmormon about how everyone has to try a dirty martini.

You may choose to change very little about your life, and you may burn every bridge you've ever crossed. Don't focus on "right or wrong" or "brave or cowardly." Follow the path to protect your heart and your relationships.

SEVEN

EXPLORATION

Choices of Substance

Be careful when you cast out your demons that you don't throw away the best of yourself.

—Friedrich Nietzsche

I sat on my hands in an Olive Garden in Murray, Utah, waiting for my friend to pause long enough to slip over and pass us a small package. She quickly delivered breadsticks to a table and then turned around to pour a glass of wine to the next group.

Emily and I were roommates in the Heritage Halls dorms at BYU and had remained friends in the years after. She left the church before me and always seemed three or four steps ahead in experiencing the world outside Mormonism. I nervously looked around at the dusty faux Tuscan decor, hoping to distract myself.

After sliding a basket of breadsticks onto a table, she sat across from me and Jackson. She pushed a little cloth pouch into my hand—marijuana edibles. Emily and I spent countless hours together at church, young adult activities, conference Sundays, and time at the temple performing baptisms for the dead. Now, she was my friendly neighborhood drug dealer.

I was excited to try wine and order my first latte, but my first experience with weed started as a sarcastic suggestion. While I was more interested in drinking, Jackson wanted to try cannabis. Cannabis was illegal federally and in Utah and incredibly stigmatized in my mind. I couldn't help picturing him covered in half-eaten slices of pizza, sitting on the couch playing *Call of Duty*, collecting dust and unemployment. It seemed to be the inevitable end to anyone who dared try such a heinous drug.

"Wouldn't it be funny if we got weed from Emily?" I joked one day, laughing at the irony of buying drugs from a past BYU roommate. I was surprised when my suggestion was met with an optimistic, "Sounds like a great idea!"

I recognized in myself a kind of double standard—the things I deemed "morally good," like drinking wine and wearing short shorts—were unquestioningly permissible. These choices needed little to no consideration or conversation before I moved forward. However, anything on Jackson's Exmormon bucket list (that was not on mine) was an *oh hell no*. Even though weed was legalized in a few states at that point, I still felt that smoking or ingesting cannabis would be a gateway to self-destruction.

I assumed we would try it once, and then it would be in the past—something to joke about with other Exmormons. Weed would never be a regular practice. But as we sped home on the interstate, the packet felt heavy in my jacket pocket. Once we were comfortably on the couch, we sampled the edibles and waited.

About an hour in, my stomach dropped into the balls of my feet. My heartbeat was a hummingbird, flapping wildly in my ears. When I glanced toward Jackson, there was a huge grin spread across his face, and his hands stretched comfortably behind his neck. Laying there on the soft, blue comforter of the bed, he seemed to be floating on the top of a cloud.

When he saw my face, he comforted me and helped distract me till the feeling slowly drained away. After a few hours, tears streamed from my eyes. I could finally uncover words to describe the awful, anxious moments I had experienced. "I never want to do that again. I was right; weed is horrible," I explained.

"Well," he responded carefully, "you never have to do it again. I thought it was nice, though... I liked it a lot more than drinking."

Frustrated by his reply, I straightened up and turned to look at him more carefully. After a pause, I said, "I don't think either of us should do it again."

The pins and needles of the previous moments gave way to a tense frustration that we both felt. Jackson reclined back across the bed and sighed. "I think it's completely fair if you never want to try it again, but I think I do."

In the first year we left the church, we walked the path of this conversation many times. The curves and bumps of the exchange became all too familiar. I thought drinking was fine; he thought smoking weed should be, too. I said alcohol was legal; he said more people die drinking than from weed—and by a long shot. He promised he wouldn't become a bum; I assured him he was wrong.

Jackson continued to smoke. His drug use was the definition of courteous, always in small amounts and never around me.

Communication was constant, and he always shared his thoughts and plans weeks in advance. To my surprise, he didn't lose his job, and his hands weren't glued to a video game controller. In the end, I drank more than he smoked. On the relationship scoreboard of "responsible substance usage," he is winning by a landslide.

The fear of the unknown and the stigma of an illegal drug pushed me to despise weed. My judgment and alarm were misplaced—and ultimately, the disagreement transformed my frustration into respect. I am honestly proud to be married to a person who won't sheepishly conform to my commands. What's more, his consistent communication and responsible drug use built trust in our relationship.

Seven years after leaving the church, we've mellowed out a bit. We drink one or two glasses of something once a week. In the last six months, Jackson smoked weed twice. We have two kids, and the occasions we are free from responsibility are pretty rare.

MINDFUL EXPLORATION

These rites of passage are part of leaving the church. At the time, the ship of our relationship rocked heavily back and forth on the waves of the unknown. As we knelt across from each other at the altar on our wedding day, I never imagined I would someday sit across from Jackson with a bong between us. There was no way I could've pictured him holding my hair as I vomited uncontrollably after drinking too much.

Experiencing something like this with my spouse was terrifying. It also made us stronger. I learned more about myself; we discovered more about each other. I sympathetically reflect on my worries from the time and recognize the necessity of this struggle.

Leaving the church will often create some level of identity crisis and relationship crisis.

Most Mormon minds are utterly devoid of any knowledge about substances. We are conditioned to believe that few things are as wicked as drugs. Most active Mormons couldn't tell you anything about drinking or drugs. As a kid, I thought coffee tables were immoral. My parents never drank, none of my friends drank, and I was a proud DARE representative in high school.

As I've watched many friends leave the church after me, drinking and drugs are a hurdle many mark as an important emblem. To be clear, you never need to drink alcohol or sip from a cup of coffee to qualify as an Exmormon. Substances may have little to do with leaving the church for some individuals.

Some of my Exmormon friends wait years before trying a glass of wine. Some buy a coffee machine and immediately incorporate a cup into their morning routine. As suggested in chapter five, following the steps for new experiences is an excellent way to decide if you are ready for different substances (see page 101). If you are curious, begin with researching, learning, and planning. Discuss with a trusted, open-minded friend. Share your decision with others, if needed. Sample the experience, then reflect.

If you feel a sense of apprehension, investigate why. In my self-reflection and discussions with others, Exmormons often hesitate to take steps outside of Mormon standards because they fear the unknown. The morality of Mormonism is a very comforting safety blanket, and the world outside can look frigidly cold. Make decisions with confidence and conviction, not out of fear and trepidation. I've enjoyed many first-time cocktails with friends freshly out of the church. Typically, they haven't tried this new experience because they need someone to support and guide them emotionally.

Addiction is another common fear. I've heard Mormons toss around the word alcoholic to describe anyone who drinks a glass of wine once a week. I assumed the first time I tried a substance, I would be immediately hooked. That is not usually how addiction works, but it doesn't mean you should be wary.

Addiction is a genuine problem, and before trying any substance for the first time, you should research and learn the risk factors. As stated in other portions of the book, consider your current mental state before experimenting with any substance. Addiction is a powerful urge to have a drug or engage in certain habits despite substantial harm and other adverse life consequences. What's more, some people are prone to addiction. Mormonism provides strong guardrails against making common mistakes associated with substances.

You may have heard friends exclaim they are "addicted" to coffee, but this is the same as saying "I'm depressed" when you are a bit melancholy for a few days. Addiction and depression are both clinical terms used by many people to express normal, day-to-day emotions. Addiction is when you will destroy your life and well-being to continue participating in drug use. Drug dependency is when someone cannot function normally without substance use.

A support network is also vital to mental health, so be wary of substances if you don't have loved ones to support. There's a big difference between getting a cocktail with your friends and drinking liquor from the bottle alone at home. Don't turn to substances as an escape.

As you survey your desire to partake in a particular substance, always consider the risks. Smoking tobacco is very addictive, and consistent use can give you lung cancer. Driving drunk is dangerous and irresponsible. If you are a woman and even for some men, getting inebriated in public or with people you don't know well can lead to victimization. These new experiences come with inherent risks. Research, planning, and personal introspection are essential.

The more research and reading you can devote to these new experiences, the better. This will help you feel at ease once you decide to try something new and prepare you to know what to expect. Speaking from first-hand experience, buying coffee beans, talking to a bartender, and navigating a Starbucks menu is legitimately intimidating. I sat in a coffee shop on my computer several times before I finally dared to nervously walk up to the counter and awkwardly order from the menu.

In my book, which you are currently reading, trying different substances is neither good nor bad. The "good, better, best" mantra constantly rang through my head as a Mormon. Everything in life can be scored on the Mormon righteousness index; nothing is amoral. My experiences with substances were world-opening, enlightening, and sometimes mind-altering.

For those who wonder, for those who are curious: try it.

For those who fear it: analyze the root of the fear.

For those who are electrified: cautiously take it a step at a time.

REFLECT AND WRITE

- How do you feel about trying new experiences outside the norms or expectations you've grown up with?
- Can you identify any double standards in your life? Are there things you consider "morally good" without much thought while opposing other choices without much consideration?
- How does communication and trust play a role in your relationships? What struggles do you anticipate when discussing and making choices about substances?
- Can you recall when you had positive and negative experiences with something? Is there an experience where, despite the risks, the rewards made it worthwhile for you? What did you learn?

The remainder of this chapter contains a breakdown of different substances, including advice on how much to take when starting out, risks and statistics, the typical culture surrounding enjoyment, and suggested further reading.

A final disclaimer: The following outlined substances are either legal or are broadly considered as or less dangerous than tobacco products or alcohol, according to the current science. The following is not medical advice, and I strongly suggest you seek other sources for further education. Be aware people can have different reactions to the same substance. If you are on medication, this is especially true. I do not claim to be an authority. Education does not equal endorsement. The following in no way is an exhaustive resource for learning. Please pursue additional research as you begin your experimentation.

ALCOHOL

Alcohol is made all over the world from countless versions of ingredients and production styles. Drinking preferences are up to personal taste and interest. You'll gain favorites with trial and error. The varieties described in the next pages are a broad generalization and do not represent a complete list. Sample something from each category to understand your likes and dislikes.

For most people, drinking is the definition of fun. As you drink, you progress from sober to buzzed, to tipsy, to drunk. At each stage, you feel more uninhibited. I usually feel numb in the extremities, and I get increasingly silly and unhinged. Being drunk doesn't usually change who you are as a person. Typically, you are more likely to show the parts of yourself you usually hold back.

To avoid getting drunk, stick to one drink per hour metric. You'll usually start "feeling it" around the 30-minute mark, but depending on body size and tolerance, you may or may not feel anything with one drink. Drinking water can also offset the effects of alcohol; if you feel it too much, stop and drink water. Drinking on an empty stomach will cause you to feel the effects much more quickly; eat a meal before starting to drink.

Never drive under the influence. Always make a plan for travel if you are planning on drinking. Drunk driving accidents are often fatal, and you put yourself and everyone else on the road at risk. Opt for a sober, designated driver or use a rideshare. You can also give yourself enough time to drink water and wait for the effects to wear off. When in doubt, do not get behind the wheel.

Drinking at home with a friend is a great alternative, especially for a beginner. Only accept drinks from people you know. If someone wants to buy you a drink, make sure the bartender hands you the drink, not the stranger. Always keep an eye on your drink. Stay with your group of friends and have a plan to meet back up if you get separated.

For your first time ordering drinks: Choose a smaller bar in town where it's not too busy. Weeknights are less crowded than weekends. Some bars are packed, and getting the bartender's attention is hard, which can be intimidating. You can either ask the bartender to make a particular cocktail or for the bartender to suggest something to you.

You can also let the bartender know you're new to drinking and you would like to sample something he suggests. Be prepared for the bartender to ask about your taste preferences. You could say, "I like sweeter drinks," or "Can you make me something more smoky and savory." Always tip your bartender. This is typically $1 to $2 per drink or 15% to 20% of your bill.

Drinking is fun until it's not. Don't overdo it. For me, drinking is fun when you get tipsy and stop drinking. After one or two drinks, you may get a nice warm feeling accompanied by feeling a little silly. If you get too drunk, things can go wrong quickly. You may end up throwing up, starting an argument, or making a choice you regret. Be aware of how you are pacing yourself and how you're feeling.

In front of Mormons: I didn't drink in front of my mom till I was out of the church for over a year. I ordered a drink at a restaurant and paid for it myself. While your family is still getting used to you leaving the church, it will probably be the easiest for them if you forgo drinking in their presence. However, if you want to give them a big "fuck you," then you're welcome to put this advice to the side.

Beer

Alcohol Content

About 5% alcohol

Average-sized man
4-5 beers to get drunk

Average-sized woman
4-5 beers to get drunk

Made from grain, hops, yeast, and water. Usually more savory and bitter than sweet, like drinking bread.

Popular Varieties

- Lagers
  Light and easy to drink
- Stouts
  Thick and malty
- Pale Ales
  Bitter and creamy
- Sours
  Some acidity and funky flavors

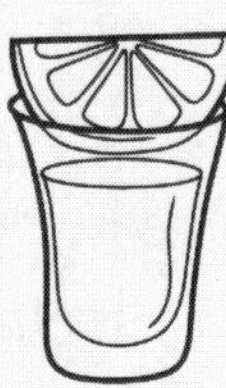

Liquor/Spirits

Alcohol Content

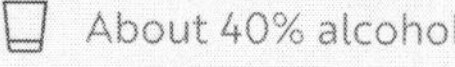

About 40% alcohol

Average-sized man
4-5 shots to get drunk

Average-sized woman
3-4 shots to get drunk

Made from ingredients that have been fremented and then distilled. If you drink it straight, the strongest taste for first-time drinkers is the "burn" of the alcohol itself, which has a chemical taste.

Popular Varieties

- Whiskey
  Smoky, nutty, oaky
- Rum
  Woody, sugary, vanilla, molasses
- Vodka
  Flavorless other than alcohol
- Gin
  Herbal, pine, juniper, sweet
- Tequila
  Toasty, sweet, and earthy

Wine

Alcohol Content — About 12% alcohol

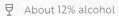

Average-sized man
3-4 glasses to get drunk

Average-sized woman
2-3 glasses to get drunk

Made from fermented grapes and can be red, white, pink, and/or sparkling. Usually more sour and sweet, with a sharper taste than grape juice.

Popular Varieties

- Reds (sweet and dark)
  Cabernet Sauvignon, Merlot, Pinot Noir, Malbec
- Whites (crisp and fruity)
  Chardonnay, Sauvignon Blanc, Pinot Gris
- Sparkling (creamy and airy)
  Champagne, Prosecco, Rosé

Cocktails

Alcohol Content — Varies by cocktail

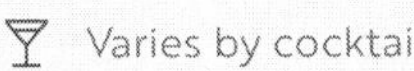

Average-sized man
Usually 2-3 to get drunk

Average-sized woman
Usually 1-2 to get drunk

Cocktails are mixed drinks made from liquor and other ingredients like juices or soda. Cocktails come in all flavors and are often sugary or flavorful enough to disguise the taste of alcohol altogether.

Popular Varieties

- Margarita
  Tequila, lime, salt, sugar
- Moscow Mule
  Vodka, ginger beer
- Old Fashioned
  Whiskey, bitters, sugar
- Martini
  Gin, vermouth, olive
- Mimosa
  Champagne, orange juice
- Mojito
  Rum, club soda, mint, lime

I think it's more polite if you don't bring alcohol into a Mormon home. Don't expect them to pay for your drinks at a restaurant (even if they want to pay for the rest of the meal). Avoid getting noticeably tipsy or drunk in front of them since this makes most Mormons very uncomfortable (though my dad—a convert—thinks it's kind of funny).

COFFEE

Similarly to alcohol, coffee is an acquired taste. And similarly to cocktails, the simplest way to experience coffee as a beginner is with lots of added sugar. Most drinks at Starbucks or Dutch Bros. will do, and I suggest you order a mocha for your first drink. A mocha is a hot chocolate with added coffee and is easy to drink for a first-timer. A latte is an excellent second option; the milk helps balance out the robust coffee flavor.

Soon, however, just as the Mormons warned, you'll be "addicted," and suddenly, the watery coffee at the car dealership or doctor's office will taste like manna from heaven. Some people only drink one cup of coffee a day; I usually drink two. I enjoy one in the morning with breakfast and another around 2 p.m. for a solid midday jolt of energy.

Tea is another forbidden beverage worth sampling. I love chai lattes, which you can usually order at a coffee shop. Green tea has health benefits and is a perfect option if you want slightly less caffeine than your average cup of coffee. Make certain your tea leaves are fresh since this can make a significant difference in taste. Invest in an electric kettle for faster tea preparation. Create a tea ritual, and pair it with a book or favorite TV show.

While you're buying your kettle, consider purchasing a coffee maker. Keurig coffee is convenient and easy to make. You put a coffee pod into the chamber, press a button, and the coffee is poured. This is basically the fast-food version of coffee. It is quickly made and low quality, but it gets the job done. I used a Keurig at home for the first years of coffee drinking.

A coffee maker with a pot is the next-level option. Brewed coffee takes slightly longer to prepare each morning and typically produces a larger portion. It also tastes much better than Keurig coffee. Coffee pots are also less expensive and better for the environment because you only buy beans rather than plastic pods. The gold standard is an espresso machine, but it is also the most costly option. Espresso is pronounced "ES-press-o," not "EX-press-o." Breville makes a wonderful espresso machine, but it will set you back at least $600.

The chart on the next page outlines the most popular espresso coffee shop drinks. Though the names may strike you as intimidating, the components are typically differing combinations of espresso, steamed milk, and water. When you go to a coffee shop, you can also ask for a "drip coffee," which is your typical diner-style coffee brewed in a pot with hot water (similar to an americano, which is espresso with hot water).

Coffee and caffeine can make you anxious and jittery, especially if you drink too much. It can make your heart race, give you indigestion, make you feel dizzy, and give you a headache. Coffee is also a diuretic, and you may need the restroom more than usual. If you drink too much coffee and feel sick, drink lots of water and eat a filling meal. Avoid drinking coffee in the evening, as it will keep you from falling asleep. You can also switch to decaffeinated coffee, which does not contain the added caffeine.

For your first time at a coffee shop: After reading this section, prepare your order and anticipate the size. Don't worry if they have the drink; all coffee shops can make the drinks I've described here. I suggest choosing a local coffee shop rather than a chain like Starbucks. Local coffee shops typically employ baristas who are very knowledgeable and operate with more flair. They can make great suggestions for first-timers. At small coffee shops, tip $1 to $2 for your drink. At chain stores, they do not usually expect a tip.

You will usually give them your name as you order, and then you step off to the side or find a chair while they make your drink. When they call your name, step up and get your drink. If you want additions, they typically have milk, sugar, lids, and other needs at a small station near the counter. Once you get your drink, you can sit down and enjoy the scenery. Mormons do not know what they're missing when it comes to coffee shops. The vibes at a solid local coffee shop are always immaculate. It's a stellar place for completing work on the computer or reading your favorite book about leaving the Mormon church.

In front of Mormons: Members are much more relaxed around coffee than alcohol for obvious reasons. Many Mormons love the smell of coffee. Honestly, you're doing them a favor by picking up a latte on the way to hang out. Most members have spent time around coffee in the workplace, so it's just less intimidating. Coffee is one gateway to quietly asserting your new identity to your family. Coffee doesn't usually ruffle feathers like mini skirts or beer, but it still sends the message: "No longer Mormon!"

TOBACCO

Tobacco usage also comes in many forms, from smoking to vaping to chewing. Smoking cigarettes and vaping are the most common versions. Nicotine is a stimulant that releases adrenaline, giving smokers a kind of buzzy, happy feeling. The first time smoking may make you nauseous and ill; sometimes, users may feel a burning sensation in the lungs and throat.

Tobacco is one of the most addictive substances. Studies show tobacco is more difficult to quit than heroin. The nicotine in tobacco makes smoking addictive, and many people struggle to quit once they begin the habit. Be aware that it is difficult to only "smoke every once in a while." Daily smokers reported smoking about 14 cigarettes per day.

While I have my morning coffee and enjoy a glass of wine with dinner a few times every week, I have always stayed clear of tobacco. I refuse to make tobacco use a habit. My grandma is a lifelong smoker and is currently fighting lung cancer. Be aware if you begin this habit, you will likely have a lifelong dependence of some kind. With that being said, if you are still interested in trying out smoking, read on.

For your first time smoking: To smoke a cigarette, use a lighter to ignite the non-filtered side of the cigarette. Put the lit cigarette (filter side) to your lips. Suck the air lightly through your mouth like a straw. Do this slowly, and only bring in a little air at a time to avoid feeling nauseous. Allow the smoke to cool as it enters your mouth by holding it in your mouth, then pulling it into your lungs. Take the cigarette out of your mouth and exhale.

Vaping is a solid alternative to smoking cigarettes or cigars. While it is better for you, it is still not safe. Vaping is cheaper than smoking and allows you to enjoy nicotine without inhaling cigarette tar. It can also preserve your sense of taste and smell and is not as harsh on your lungs. That being said, vaping is still addictive and can lead to serious health complications.

In front of Mormons and everyone else too: Smoking around those who don't smoke is typically considered rude and inconsiderate, and smoking indoors in most places in the United States is illegal. Secondhand smoke puts other's health at risk, especially children and those with other health complications. If you are a smoker or may become one, it's best to smoke outdoors away from other people. This way, you can enjoy it without risking anyone else's health.

CANNABIS

Weed, cannabis, marijuana, and pot—a drug of many names. Cannabis is a well-loved drug and gives most users a calm, relaxed feeling. Cannabis comes from a plant; the user ingests or smokes the dried bud. The effects of cannabis vary depending on the user. For many, feeling stoned allows the user to feel happy and chill. However, for some, it can have the opposite effect. Cannabis usually makes my heart race and makes me acutely aware of my anxiety. Although, every third or fourth time I try it, I have a good experience. For Jackson, cannabis delivers a sweet, calming happiness.

As with the other substances listed in this chapter, safe experimentation is recommended. It's impossible to know how you'll react to any substance till you try it. Ensuring a purposeful set (your mindset) and setting (your environment) can significantly impact your ability to enjoy the experience. Experiment with cannabis in a situation where you feel entirely at ease. Trying it out at a chaotic party or a loud concert isn't the best choice for a first-timer.

At the time of writing this book, cannabis is still federally illegal. Many states have legalized medicinal cannabis, and twenty-one states have legalized recreational cannabis. In my experience, most Mormons view cannabis as more disagreeable than alcohol or tobacco. This is ironic, considering alcohol and tobacco are wildly worse for your health. Alcohol and tobacco are also much more addictive and dependency-forming when compared to cannabis. Many, many more deaths are attributed to tobacco use and alcohol use than cannabis.

While alcohol use increases the likelihood of violence, addiction, cancer, brain damage, and death from overdose—cannabis does none of these things. Cannabis may be an excellent alternative to prescription painkillers like OxyContin, which are also incredibly addictive. Cannabis, however, can be habit-forming. Moderation is vital to reduce risk.

Ways to enjoy it: There are many different ways to enjoy cannabis, and most people develop a preference. Some of the most popular versions include smoking, eating, and vaping. You can experience cannabis using a bong, joint, vape, edibles, tinctures, oils, and pills.

I recommend edibles for those who don't want to smoke. Edibles can be hard to dose, especially if you make them yourself or it's your first time experiencing cannabis. If possible, buy packaged edibles with the dosage clearly labeled from a legal state. If you know a friend traveling to a legal state, you can ask them to pick some up for you. Start your THC at 5mg, and ramp up from there. For larger people or those looking to get higher on the first go-round, start at 10mg.

It takes between thirty minutes and two hours to notice the effects. Edibles mean you ingest the THC, which means the high lasts longer. The high can last six hours for some, and others feel it for up to 24 hours. Get high on a Friday night or Saturday when nothing is planned for the following day. Do not get high for the first time when you have work or school the next day.

Vaping, joints, spliffs, and bongs are all ways to smoke weed. Smoking is a convenient way to enjoy cannabis because the effects are briefer. The THC is absorbed through your lungs, and you can expect to be high for a few hours. Time spent high can vary widely based on weight, tolerance, dosage, concentration, and delivery method. In my experience, bongs deliver a very intense hit. Vaping is more measured and smooth. Expect to cough for your first few times smoking. Smoking cannabis can irritate the back of your throat, especially for newbies, and if you allow the hot air down your windpipe too quickly.

How to find cannabis: If you live in a legal state, you can go to your local dispensary. Ask the person at the counter to recommend a few products. Plan to tell them how you want to take it—smoking, vaping, edibles, or any other method—and what type of experience you want.

Sativa is known to be mind-enhancing and good for pain relief. Indica is known for relieving anxiety and is more relaxing. While some people swear by a particular strain of weed, these claims may not be valid for everyone. Try experimenting with different types of strains to find what suits you best.

SATIVA

High CBD Levels

Effects: Energizing, stimulating, reduces anxiety, increases creativity

Suggested for daytime use

INDICA

High THC Levels

Effects: Relaxing, pain relief, decreases nausea, better sleep

Suggested for nighttime use

HYBRID

Mixed

Effects: Sativa and Indica effects depending on parent strains

Many states only allow medical cannabis prescribed by a doctor. If you live in one of these states, you can request a prescription for chronic pain. Some states only allow a prescription if you are diagnosed with specific ailments, like seizures or PTSD. Talk to your doctor and explain why you need medical cannabis.

For those who want to enjoy cannabis recreationally but do not live in a legal state, you'll have to get a little more creative.

Most people—even Mormons—know someone who smokes weed. Anyone with more than five tattoos, piercings, blue hair, or who wears 80s rock band t-shirts can probably help you find cannabis. Usually, if they don't know anyone, they will know someone who knows someone who can sell to you.

Buying drugs can be intimidating and make you feel quite mysterious and edgy. I suggest using an app like Telegram, which encrypts messages and stores your information on a secure server. When meeting someone you don't know, always take a friend. Finding a "plug" (someone who sells drugs) that a friend recommends goes a long way because you know your friend trusts them. Meet in a relatively public place, like a park, where you can be more or less alone while still having people around. Take steps to stay safe, especially if you are a woman.

In front of Mormons and everyone else too: Enjoy cannabis privately, and avoid getting high around others who are not smoking. It's simply bad form to get high around others who are not high. Mormons and non-Mormons often feel uncomfortable around cannabis if they are not smokers because it is federally illegal. Part of being a drug user is learning to enjoy discreetly and in a setting where you and others can feel at ease.

PSYCHEDELICS

If alcohol and tobacco are familiar, and cannabis is taboo, psychedelics fall further down the spectrum of the unknown. As a member of the church, I believed LSD and heroin were basically the same—equally horrible. Psychedelics genuinely belong in a class of their own. These psychoactive drugs are quite different from drinking or cigarettes.

Before you skip this section and think, "There's no way I'll ever try psychedelics," at least read the section! I promise reading can't hurt you. Of all the substances listed in this chapter, psychedelics are the only category that truly deserves consideration. If you abstain from drinking, cannabis, and even coffee, I hope you'll give thought to trying psychedelics.

Psychedelics are hallucinogenic drugs that create an altered state of consciousness. These "trips" can produce intense visual effects and physical sensations. Tripping can feel dream-like and euphoric, and many people who experience psychedelics report feelings of acute mental and spiritual clarity.

Tripping can be highly visual, and everything around you appears to move with energy and life. Thoughts and feelings become clear and potent. And, as cliche as it sounds, you feel at peace with everything around you and the universe.

The experiences I've had on psychedelics have been life-altering in the best way. As someone who has struggled with depression my whole life, magic mushrooms did more for me in a single night than a year of taking antidepressants.

Sam Harris's writing helped me understand the use case for psychedelics. He is a neuroscientist and philosopher, and this quote is from his essay "Drugs and the Meaning of Life." You can easily find the whole essay online.

Harris explains, "I have two daughters who will one day take drugs. Of course, I will do everything in my power to see that they choose their drugs wisely, but a life lived entirely without drugs is neither foreseeable nor, I think, desirable. I hope they someday enjoy a morning cup of tea or coffee as much as I do. If they drink alcohol as adults, as they probably will, I will encourage them to do it safely. If they choose to smoke marijuana, I will urge moderation.

"Tobacco should be shunned, and I will do everything within the bounds of decent parenting to steer them away from it. Needless to say, if I knew that either of my daughters would eventually develop a fondness for methamphetamine or crack cocaine, I might never sleep again. But if they don't try a psychedelic like psilocybin (magic mushrooms) or LSD at least once in their adult lives, I will wonder whether they had missed one of the most important rites of passage a human being can experience."

This quote perfectly encapsulates my feelings toward each drug he lists, especially psychedelics. I spent two and a half decades hearing about the transformative powers of the Holy Ghost. I've felt peace in the temple, I've felt elated joy while singing, and I've cried during intense prayer. With that said, no spiritual experience in Mormonism matches the powerful transcendent nature of psychedelics.

While I was hesitant to include psychedelics in this chapter, it felt like a crime to leave it out. Societal norms dictating which substances are acceptable and which substances are objectionable have no basis in real risk, harm, and reward. I am astounded that alcohol is legal and normalized while mushrooms are illegal and demonized. Countless deaths and acts of abuse have happened due to alcohol consumption. The harm done by psychedelics is minuscule by comparison.

There are many different versions of psychedelics, each producing various types of trips. LSD lasts eight to twelve hours, is very cerebral, and has a focusing effect. Magic mushrooms last four to six hours, create more visual effects and induce more of a full-body trip. DMT, peyote, ayahuasca, and mescaline are other popular types of psychedelics. Most new psychonauts gravitate toward LSD or Magic Mushrooms. There's something gleeful about going from LDS to LSD.

I first tripped on magic mushrooms while lying in my bathtub in our Brooklyn apartment. It was 2018, and as I lay in the absolute dark, my fingers rose to my eyes. Though my hands were slightly numb, I could feel my eyes were leaking. I had never experienced such elevated happiness and peace. My joy wasn't because I was high or, like alcohol, because I was giddy. It was because I felt at peace with myself for the first time in memorable history.

This quiet, peaceful center inside my chest remained for months after my first trip. I recommitted to my mental and physical health. I started running again. Flowers were more beautiful than ever before. I showed more abundant kindness. While most experiences with substances are fleeting, leaving you wanting more, hungover, or nauseous—psychedelics left me in a month-long state of bliss.

Psilocybin is proven to help rewire the brain of depressed people, and I believe they had this effect on me. In recent studies, psilocybin has helped treat antidepressant-resistant depression. Clinical trials to prove these effects are underway. Hopefully, soon, these drugs will be both legal and easily accessible.

For your first time tripping: Set and setting are essential when trying psychedelics. This is true not only for the first time but also for the twentieth. Ensure you are in a peaceful, safe place with trustworthy people. I recommend having a "trip sitter," someone to sit with you who is sober or someone who has tried the drug before and who can take the drug with you. Trip sitters make the experience more fun, introspective, and safe. A trip sitter can also sit in a room nearby and be available if you need help but not interfere if you prefer to trip alone.

LSD

LSD, known as "acid," is a small tab of paper dissolved on the tongue

Effects: Promotes euphoria, distorts vision and sound, and enhances perspective.

6-12 hours

MAGIC MUSHROOMS

Psilocybin, also known as "shrooms," are varying types of hallucinogenic mushrooms.

Effects: Promotes euphoria, distorts vision and sound, and enhances perspective.

4-6 hours

AYAHUASCA

Ceremonial brew made by boiling two plants. Contains the chemical DMT.

Effects: Users experience intense visuals and may recall past trauma very powerfully.

4-14 hours

Between 2-3 grams of dried mushrooms is a great place to start for your first time. You can eat them or grind them up and drink them with tea. If trying LSD, take a single tab. Trip on an empty stomach. Sometimes, the initial portion of a trip can make you feel nauseous, and your stomach should be empty. This will also make the trip more potent.

There are different phases of a psychedelic trip. The onset can take about thirty minutes to an hour. The "peak," the most intense part of a trip, lasts for about one to two hours on magic mushrooms and about two to three hours on LSD. After the peak is the "comedown" of the trip, which can last for two to four hours on magic mushrooms and up to 24 hours on LSD.

This is why it's wise to trip when you have no responsibilities for at least 24 hours from initially taking the drug. I prefer tripping on a Friday night (magic mushrooms) or Saturday morning (LSD) because this gives you all of Sunday to recover from your trip entirely. Turn your phone off or give it to a friend who can help with texts. Choose a good playlist for your trip, have comfort items like pillows and blankets, and access to pen and paper if you want to write something down.

Sometimes, psychedelics lead to "bad trips" where you get into a negative headspace while tripping. Sometimes, psychedelics can cause a panic attack or make the user very sad or feel unwell. To avoid a bad trip, carefully prepare by researching and knowing what to expect, find a trip sitter you trust, and avoid tripping if you are already in a dark place mentally. Psychedelics can help with depression, but if your depression has been very severe or you've been feeling suicidal, do not experiment with this class of drug.

How to find psychedelics: The steps for finding psychedelics are similar to those used to find cannabis. You usually need to ask around and find a friend with a plug. It is easier to find cannabis than psychedelics, but typically, someone who sells cannabis can help you find a place to start. Exmormons seem particularly interested in psychedelics, so reaching out to an Exmormon friend or group may point you in the right direction.

As stated with cannabis, do not put yourself in unsafe situations. If you are meeting someone, use a public area. Do not go to someone's home if you do not know them well. Use references to find someone who you can trust. If your friend already knows someone, see if they would be willing to pick it up for you rather than you going yourself.

SEEK LIFE'S WONDERS

Drugs have risks and rewards. I've had both good experiences and bad experiences while under the influence. Sometimes I have a lot of fun, and sometimes I don't. I think I always go back for more because, personally, the rewards make the risks worth it. Sometimes, I feel like I'm riding a bucking bull. If I stay on long enough, I get the payoff. If I drink too much, I get bucked off. If I'm careful, I enjoy the ride.

While I hesitate to encourage or condone drug use, I also feel my experiences are so precious it is a crime to remove this chapter from my Exmormon guide altogether. I've learned so much about myself and my mind. My humanity has blossomed and grown. I am stronger.

As with everything in this book, you are the one who finally gets to choose. Consider my voice one of many swaying you this way and that. Of course I have an opinion. Everyone does. As I've shared throughout the book, the best part of being an Exmormon is you finally get to decide for yourself.

Reading *The Book of Mormon* or sitting in conference, you never feel free to say or think, "This is bullshit advice. I disagree." In Mormonism, the doctrine is either true or you haven't prayed hard enough. Out of Mormonism, you finally have a license to agree and disagree according to the dictates of your mind.

If alcohol makes you happy, drink it. If it makes you miserable, stop. If psychedelics aren't your thing, don't do them. Your life has been and will continue to be full of people who believe they are right and true and correct. Being an Exmormon means you finally get to exercise the muscle in your brain that looks inward for affirmation and direction instead of outward. You are actually and truly a free agent.

EIGHT

SEXUALITY

Loving Yourself and Others Too

Freedom lies in being bold.

—Robert Frost

Britney Spears peered up at me, wearing a jean skirt and a cherry red button-up top. My friends yelled the lyrics to "(You Drive Me) Crazy" at a fourth-grade slumber party while I scrutinized the album cover. At eight, I already knew Britney Spears was "bad," though I couldn't have explained why. Her wide, innocent smile appeared wholesome enough, though the length of her skirt and bare thighs were a hint. As a newly baptized little girl, I had already been told to "keep my legs together" while sitting and "stop being so immodest" if my dress revealed my thighs when I played.

By the time I hit Young Women's, I finally learned the dirty word to describe what made Britney Spears so bad. She was sexy. And sexy is bad. Soon, I added Megan Fox, Christina Aguilera,

Paris Hilton, and The Spice Girls to my growing list of dangerous women. They composed a complete reference library to determine what sexy meant and how to avoid becoming sexy myself. Sexy was low-cut tops, thongs, lacy bras, and mini skirts. Sexy was also moving your hips back and forth and bending down with your butt sticking in the air.

By twelve, I was ashamed and disgusted to learn I was also sexy. This was not because I tried to copy the women in magazines—I was sexy because I possessed a female body. I was sexy because breasts happened to be part of my physical anatomy. It was my fault if the young men looked at me and had evil thoughts. When I ran a cross-country race in shorts, my body was inappropriate.

Despite my best efforts to be pure and Jesus-loving, puberty transformed me into an automatic whore. I felt embarrassed and ashamed when old men stared at me in the mall. I knew I had done something wrong to attract this attention. The massive balance sheet continued to amass in my brain—a careful ledger of how to avoid the sexiness of my body. My go-to moves were baggy clothes, continuous slouching, and avoiding anyone male.

I hated my body because by having a body, I was sin.

While my understanding of the word "sexy" was intricate and prodigious, I could barely define the word sex. Words like labia, clitoris, ejaculate, and scrotum were essentially unknown to me till I was in my twenties. Human reproductive anatomy was an absolute mystery. Euphemisms and poorly constructed analogies were all I clung to in my attempt to understand sex.

I knew everything about what it meant to be sexy and absolutely nothing about what it meant to have sex. Even in college, I refused to hold hands on a first date because I felt it made me "easy." Close-lipped pecks were the only permissible form of kissing. There was no knowledge of sexuality past these two virtuous forms of showing physical affection. The entirety of the sexual experience was to remain behind the mystifying shrouds of marriage.

When I was kissing my first real Mormon boyfriend at sixteen, he made an odd grunting noise. He suddenly seemed to be on a different planet. A moment passed. He grabbed a blanket, put it over his lap, and immediately asked me to go home. Shocked and confused, I walked back to my car. It wasn't till college that I realized what had happened.

On my mission, a companion shared she didn't want to have sex on her wedding night—she wouldn't be ready. Relieved, I admitted I felt the same way. Another friend shared a story about bleeding profusely on her wedding night and how she became so worried that her new husband drove her to the emergency room.

How could I go from tiny pecks on the cheek to sex in a single day? I couldn't even sit through the first thirty seconds of a Nicki Minaj music video without turning beet red. Anything to do with human sexuality was utterly intimidating.

Though you may physically stop attending church and wearing garments, your brain remains Mormon in many ways, and sex is no exception. Years of chastity lessons about lost virtue aren't going to go away overnight. For me, sexuality and sexual expression were the most difficult bridges to begin to cross—even now, I'm barely halfway.

I got married in the temple and am still married to the same person. I'm in a monogamous heterosexual relationship with the only person I've ever slept with. As someone who has only been with one person, my experience with sex and sexuality is limited. I've never dated outside the church or had multiple sex partners. I am not gay or trans, but the information in this chapter is still applicable to people with any orientation.

While this is my experience with sexuality as a Mormon woman, I recognize a need to share the stories of others as well. I've had many queer friends leave the church. Two of these friends, Trace and Alex, share their stories in this chapter. Their words illustrate the struggle of growing up queer in a homophobic religion, and they each explain how they overcame shame and repression. Their stories highlight the difficulty of overcoming the guilt of being queer in the church.

TRACE'S STORY

I grew up as a young man within Mormonism hearing the other side of the message Alyssa internalized. While she grew up ashamed and disgusted at the idea of being sexy, I felt similar shame and disgust at the idea of finding women sexy. Sexuality was all around me, and I hated it. I grimaced when I saw a bikini-clad woman on a billboard. I turned away in disgust at anything approaching a sex scene in a movie or even more than a bit of kissing. Anything to do with sexuality was a threat, a temptation to resist and overcome. I valued modesty and chastity, as I was taught. Noticing sexuality with anything other than disgust was a personal failing in my eyes, and I shoved all of that into a corner, figuring I'd deal with it when I was an adult.

With all that, though, I was still an adolescent boy, and hormones don't simply disappear when ignored. Whenever I fell into temptation, as I saw it, I took it badly. I felt like the most wretched person in the world. I berated myself, ruminated in guilt, and occasionally even escalated to hitting or pinching myself to try to train myself out of it. It never worked, and I found myself haunted by my weakness and self-perceived depravity throughout my adolescence and early adulthood.

I took my faith's prohibitions seriously and rarely dug where I wasn't supposed to. Still, I seem to have sublimated my romantic interests into something safely out of the realm of reality. I engaged with sexuality only through a tightly segmented-off part of my mind in an elaborate fantasy world disconnected from anything that felt too real, discovering the peculiar world of anthropomorphic art online.

So far as I can tell, the combination of my internalization of prohibitions on sexuality and the need for some sort of outlet channeled and focused my thoughts toward a deep-running interest in anthropomorphism. It was the only domain where I could hesitantly explore the idea of romance. That sphere felt somehow disconnected from the baggage, cruft, and uncertainty around a real world where I had internalized that I should clamp down on all feelings in that domain, so I lingered there.

I kept telling myself that romance would come later—that crushes and noticing interest in women and all the rest would be right around the corner. As I got older and it kept not happening, though, I started to seriously ask myself whether I was capable of being in love. It took until I left Mormonism in my early twenties for anything to change. When I stepped away from the faith and gave myself a bit of room to breathe, I noticed, gradually, a hesitant interest in men. I began to date a year or so after I left, and a year after that, I met the man who would become my husband. As soon as I started dating, and particularly when I met him, things simply felt right. Every time I hugged him or held his hand, I felt perfectly at peace. The swirl of tension and confusion around sexuality in my adolescence fell away into a comfortable security.

Many of the specifics of my experience are unusual. The broader tension between Mormonism's purity culture, male sexuality, and a world increasingly comfortable with sexuality as a whole, though, leads to peculiar struggles for many young men within the faith. Guilt and shame make these young men hesitate to voice those struggles or even think too deeply about them. I was lucky in the end. My story resolved in a tidy way when I found room to breathe away from Mormonism and settled into a stable, happy relationship with the love of my life. Even so, I'll never get those years of tension, self-hatred, and repression back.

THE SEXUAL SELF OUTSIDE MORMONISM

While covering every aspect of this topic is impossible, I hope the following pages are a good primer for those leaving the church. At the very least, I hope this chapter sets you on the path to having a positive relationship with sex as an Exmormon.

Even if you've been married or are currently married, it doesn't mean sex is straightforward. Some Mormons have sex regularly, some rarely, and some members have never had sex. And for those Mormons who identify as queer, they are taught to expect to live an entire lifetime of celibacy. Many people internalize a religious, sexual shame that parades through their minds for the rest of their lives. Investigating your past thoughts, feelings, and hangups about sexuality is a vital step to leaving them all behind.

As a new Exmormon, you may still assume marriage is superior to living with someone. You've probably internalized it's a sin to be gay, and it's great to be straight. And while the church may purport that one sexual partner is preferable to having many, you can begin to let that assumption go.

In the church, there is only one path to perfection. Out of the church, perfection is finding happiness and healthiness. If you're against a particular aspect of sex and sexuality, investigate why you feel that way. Did you arrive at that conclusion because it is truly how you feel? Instead, consider that you've been primed to feel that way by outside forces.

Mormons believe that unmarried people should not be sexual beings in any way—no masturbation, no sexual interest in a partner, and no sexual identity. While you can have crushes and go on dates, there is no discourse on how this plays into any sexual experience. Then, once you're married, your sexuality only exists within your relationship with your spouse. No pornography, no sex toys, and no sexual experiences exist beyond the body and mind of the other person.

Despite what Mormonism taught, you are a sexual being with desires, appetites, and passions. Or, maybe you're asexual, someone with little to no sexual desire or attraction. There is a vast spectrum of gender, sex, and sexuality. There is only one path presented in Mormonism, but outside the church, you can walk in whatever way feels best.

Though you may be more comfortable shoving those feelings and identities away, allow yourself to investigate instead. There iss nothing wrong with learning more about sex. The more information you have, the more likely you are to enjoy sex. There are worlds of experiences waiting past "not married" and "married."

In *The Family: A Proclamation to the World*, the church outlines the very particular and narrow definition of what makes a godly family. Women watch the children. Men make the money. The penis goes into the vagina. This is what we're meant to emulate. Anything that falls outside these bounds is wicked and unnatural. Homosexuality is renamed "same-sex attraction." The church redefines being gay as a chosen lifestyle instead of the reality of someone's existence.

Gay marriage wasn't even federally legalized till 2015. In some social groups and geographic regions, homosexuality feels as natural as breathing. However, some pockets of the country still exist where being openly gay can be outright dangerous. Society adds another layer of homophobia on top of Mormon culture.

Those who are gay or who fall somewhere outside the strict definition of heterosexuality often struggle with shame. Often, as young adults move through puberty and even as adults, there may not be an introduction to the vocabulary needed to understand what they may be experiencing. Many queer youth feel tremendously isolated and outcast, though some internet forums can be a venue for connection.

Giving words and names to feelings and identity is integral to discovering who you are. Representation and education matter. Growing up in the church, most will only have close experience with one version of gender and sexuality. Perhaps you assume you are straight or already know you are gay. You may question your identity and feel uncertain about where you fit along the scale. There are infinite configurations of sexuality and relationships, and these identities can change over time. Value the process of self-reflection and discovery over finding the proper label. Review the brief glossary of terms below. Some may be familiar; some may be new.

COMMON TERMS FOR SEXUAL ORIENTATION AND GENDER IDENTITY

Sexual Orientations

A person's pattern of emotional, romantic, and sexual attraction to a specific gender. Sexual orientation is your preference for a specific gender.

Heterosexual: when an individual is attracted to the opposite sex

Gay: men who are attracted to men

Lesbian: women who are attracted to women

Pansexual: attraction to people regardless of their gender identity

Bisexual: attraction to men and women and more than one gender

Asexual: a person who experiences little or no sexual attraction

Gender Identity

A person's deeply held belief about their gender. This identity may be the same or different from what was assigned to them at birth.

Cisgender: when a person's gender identity is the same as the sex registered at birth

Transgender: a term for everybody whose gender differs from the sex and gender that they were assigned at birth

Non-Binary: people who don't identify as male or female

Intersex: a person born with genitalia or reproductive organs that aren't clearly "male" or "female"

LGBTQIA+

This acronym stands for Lesbian, Gay, Bisexual, Transgender, and Queer. The plus at the end indicates this term includes all other identities not expressly mentioned in the first five terms. It is often used as an inclusive term for anyone who is not cisgender and heterosexual.

Queer: An umbrella term for people who are not heterosexual or cisgender. This term is also shorthand for members of the LGBTQIA+ community.

Other Important Terms Relating to Sex

Sexually Transmitted Infections (STIs): Infections that can be transmitted through sexual contact. Common STIs include HIV, herpes, chlamydia, gonorrhea, syphilis, and HPV.

Masturbation: Self-stimulation of one's genitals for sexual pleasure and exploration.

Polyamory: The practice of having multiple consensual romantic or sexual relationships simultaneously with the knowledge and consent of all involved parties.

Monogamy: A relationship structure in which individuals have only one sexual or romantic partner at a time.

Safe Sex: Practices that reduce the risk of STIs and unintended pregnancies, such as condom use and regular STI testing.

GOOD SEX

Horror stories of wedding night sex were passed around BYU and my mission like trading cards. A favorite was a tale of a new husband who could not wait till after the reception to have sex. The first time is in a car between the temple ceremony and the reception. The sex lasts seconds, and the bride holds back tears while still in her white gown. The groom, red-faced and panting, smiles from ear to ear.

Fear and anxiety bubbled up in me whenever I heard these stories, though they were always shared in this sly, humorous manner. A combination of "Isn't it funny they're so excited to have sex" and "Isn't uninformed virginity hilarious?" Well, Brother Daniels, it's time to wake up. Uninformed virginity isn't hilarious. It's actually terrifying, especially for women.

Usually, this flavor of sex only leads to one orgasm. On average, it takes a man five minutes to ejaculate, though under thirty seconds is also possible. A woman needs fifteen to twenty minutes on average. Unfortunately, humans are already at an evolutionary mismatch for great sex in heterosexual relationships. Add the religious shame, and you've got a recipe for disaster.

The fault lies not with the new bride or even the overly excited groom—it lies with a culture and religion devoid of any practical sex education. What happens in a relationship where neither party understands much at all about their own body or the body of their partner? What happens when sex is so taboo that even seeking information about your body feels wrong or immoral? And what happens when young men and young women know so little about consent that some level of sexual harm is almost guaranteed?

Information on healthy and great sex fills many books and magazines. However, it is an elusively taboo topic, even for nonmembers. There are some basics you did not explicitly learn about in Young Men's and Young Women's. Fundamentals of good sex are pretty simple and apply to all genders and sexualities.

Whether you have been married for years or never had sex, revisiting these ideas and standards leads to a more pleasurable, healthier sex life. I've compiled the following information from personal experience and research. I am not an (s)expert by any means. Research and investigate outside the information presented here.

Informed Consent. Good sex always starts with informed consent. Consent is more than a single "yes" or "no." Anyone can recount a time they said yes but actually meant no, or vice versa. Consent is informed when the individual is competent and can understand what they're consenting to. Consent is an unambiguous and conscious decision to engage in a mutually agreed-upon activity. Sex without consent is called rape. Sexual contact without consent is called sexual assault. Rape and sexual assault can happen within a marriage or committed relationship. Someone under the influence of drugs or alcohol is unable to consent.

Consent does not have to be awkward. Some have shared that asking for consent feels forced or embarrassing. You can create a setting where asking for consent and receiving consent feels natural. Honestly, creating a safe, consensual setting for sex is sexier than just about anything else. Use humor and playfulness. Incorporate asking for consent into your foreplay. You can say, "I would really love this. How do you feel about it?"

WHEN GIVING OR ASKING FOR CONSENT, REMEMBER FRIES

Freely given: The other person wants to participate without pressure or coercion. There should be no guilt or obligation involved in sex.

Reversible: Consent can be revoked at any time and for any reason. If the other person changes their mind and says no to a specific activity, the sexual contact must end immediately. Changing your mind halfway through is allowed.

Informed: The involved parties should know exactly what they are consenting to. Boundaries, expectations, and the nature of the sexual activity should be discussed.

Enthusiastic: Consent should be eager and optimistic. Consent is not an absence of the word "no." Verbal and nonverbal cues should show excitement and willingness.

Specific: Consent for one sexual activity, like a blow job, does not mean consent for another sexual activity, like penetrative sex. Each new act requires specific consent.

Accept the decision immediately if your partner sets a boundary or changes their mind. Nothing builds trust in a sexual relationship like someone respecting the boundaries of consent. When you listen to your partner, they know you respect them. Check-in throughout a sexual encounter to ensure continued consent. You can say, "Are you okay?" and "Do you want to keep going?"

Consent is the basis for healthy, happy, and good sex. You cannot have good sex without a baseline feeling of safety. Prioritize practicing this skill.

Communication. We assume a lot about sex from movies, television, and pornography. In the average sex scene, a steamy makeout session turns into the two simultaneously taking each other's clothes off. After a few moments of heavy breathing and grunting, both moan loudly and fall, panting, back to each side of the bed. Viola, without a single word between them, both are extraordinarily satisfied.

While I hate to bear bad news, this is unrealistic. Good sex requires significant physical and verbal communication. Before having sex, share what turns you on, what you don't like, and your specific desires. If you don't know what turns you on, head to the masturbation section later in this chapter.

While having sex, be prepared to be direct and explain what feels good and what does not. This can be as simple as "Right there is perfect," "A little slower," or "Let's try a different position." After sex, talk about what you liked and didn't like. You can explain, "I really liked when you..." or "Next time, let's skip..." Communicate before, during, and after sex.

Nothing feels vulnerable in the way sex does. Some people might fake an orgasm to make their partner feel good or excited. You might say yes to sex because you don't want to hurt your partner's feelings. You may be embarrassed when you orgasm before your partner. If you struggle to help your partner orgasm, that doesn't mean you are "bad at sex." It only means you are still learning about each other. Instead of being embarrassed, listen to what they need. Talk to each other.

Bad sex happens when either party conceals how they are feeling. Sex should always be enjoyable for both parties. You should never have sex solely to make someone else happy. Some people avoid sharing true desires or interests for fear of judgment. Building trust through open, positive communication will support long-term sexual happiness.

Self-love. If you ever want to love someone, love yourself unconditionally first. Finding happiness in your own skin is difficult—this goes for your body and soul. Individuals who report the highest level of body satisfaction also report the highest levels of sexual satisfaction. This doesn't mean you have to be model-level hot; it simply means you feel happy in your body. Focusing on pleasure is difficult when you only think about how your thighs look. Regular exercise, eating healthily, and grooming are simple ways to start caring for and loving your body.

Focus on your soul and mind. Poor mental health affects libido; it is hard to relax and enjoy yourself sexually if your mind is plagued by negativity, anxiety, or depression. Engaging in a mindfulness practice like meditation is a powerful way to center yourself daily. Going to talk therapy improves mental wellness—when you're going through a faith transition, therapy will have a massive impact on your ability to cope.

Part of self-love is enjoying the journey of sex and having a good sense of humor about all the aspects of sex. Mormonism makes sex an intensely serious endeavor. Sex used to be for procreation and sanctioned only by God through an eternal marriage. Throw all that away. Sex can be for fun.

There's a surprising amount of awkwardness and silliness involved in sex as people and couples begin to figure out what works for them. Sex can be hot and heavy, or it can be funny and clumsy. Sex involves strange noises, bodily fluids, and unhinged feelings. While you're working on self-love, develop a sense of humor. As long as you're enjoying yourself, don't take the awkward moments too seriously.

Sex Logistics. Many a sex life has improved through communication and body positivity, but lube may win first prize in the "Best Sex Enhancer" competition. Lubrication is gel or liquid applied to the genitals before and during sex. It reduces friction and elevates pleasure for men and women. Vaginal dryness can make sex painful for women, and the likelihood of dryness increases as a woman ages. Lube can be water- silicon- or oil-based; try different types to see which works best. Use lube even if you don't think you need it—it makes a difference.

Incorporating toys into your sex life can add extra fun and pleasure. Vibrators, dildos, harnesses, cock rings, and sleeves are common categories of sex toys. These can be used for solo sex or sex with a partner. Foreplay is an essential element of sex, and using sex toys can allow both parties to enjoy a sexual experience for a more extended period. Your partner may be hesitant to use sex toys. Respect his, her, or their boundaries. Sex is intimidating for many people, and it is expected to be nervous about integrating something new.

Protection. Condoms are an indispensable element of sex and should always be used when having sex with a new partner. Most people know condoms prevent pregnancy. Condoms also prevent sexually transmitted diseases and infections from passing from one partner to another. You should use a condom even if you or your partner are on hormonal birth control, like an IUD. Use condoms for vaginal, oral, and anal sex. If someone tries to pressure you into sex without a condom, it's a massive billboard communicating that they do not respect your boundaries. You should not have sex with them.

STD testing is another critical aspect of protection. The CDC recommends testing at least once a year. With multiple partners, the CDC recommends testing every three to six months. Depending on the type of STD, testing can involve a urine sample, mouth swab, or blood sample. If a potential sex partner has an STD, you may be unable to tell. This is why using a condom is vital, because even if someone tells you they've been tested, there may be no way to know for sure.

Most of the time, STDs have no apparent symptoms, or the symptoms are delayed. You can get an STD from oral, anal, or vaginal sex. Brief sexual contact of any kind can transmit STDs. Many cities and states offer free testing, especially for men who have sex with men. Do not avoid testing due to fears of expensive medical tests. Go to your local Pride Center or research online to see what resources are available in your area. Alternatively, talk to your doctor if you may have an STD and about STD prevention.

DATING AND SEX OUTSIDE THE CHURCH

Leaving the church as a single adult can be nerve-racking. The church has countless rules and social customs surrounding dating and courtship. As a Mormon, you meet potential dates at church dances and in single adult wards. The young man always initiates and pays for dates.

Mormons never ask for sex or start dropping hints about blow jobs. There are no expectations of staying the night after a date. While sex is off limits, many Mormons will discuss marriage after the second or third date—I had conversations about marriage with boys I dated before I turned eighteen.

While dating church culture is old-fashioned and sexist, it can also be reassuring. Rules are comforting because shared expectations are abundantly clear. The steps to success are drawn in stone, and the church has courtship down to a Michalangelo-level sculpture.

Once you leave the church, the structure and the shared expectations disappear. When the promise of a shared value system disappears, all bets are off. Culturally, in the United States, most people expect to have sex within the first few months of dating. It is safe to assume some people expect sex on the first date. New Exmormons may be unprepared for how quickly the topic and question of sex comes up in mainstream dating. Anticipate this as your new reality since it can be easy to be blindsided by this after growing up in an abstinence-only culture. Draw personal boundaries on how far you want to go and when this will happen in your relationships.

As with many challenging phases in life, give yourself time to learn the new you before pursuing a relationship outside the church. Reassess yourself and define what you want from dating before downloading Tinder and starting to swipe. What are you looking for in a relationship? What types of experiences do you hope for? What do you want on a physical level, and how can you communicate that with someone else? Prepare to proceed at your own pace, and find someone who won't pressure you to go any faster.

When you meet someone impatient with or dismissive of your boundaries, it means it's time to move on. Be open and honest, and prepare to stand firm in your decision. Maybe someone you meet is looking for sex on the first date, and you also want that. If you don't, clearly and directly explain your boundaries. This goes for both men and women—if you meet someone who denigrates your preferences and boundaries, they are no good for you.

Once you set a boundary, do your absolute best to be as clear-headed as possible when meeting someone new. It is astonishingly easy to hold your boundaries when you meet someone you are disinterested in. However, you may meet someone you fall head-over-heels for, and then you must decide what to do.

Infatuation and love are not the same, but they often feel the same, especially initially. If you add sex to infatuation, I sure hope you are with someone who will treat you respectfully and kindly. Sometimes, we find ourselves obsessed with someone who is not suitable for us at all. You may find yourself kicking your boundaries to the curb in the heat of a moment and then feeling regret the next day or week.

As you set a boundary, consider how you'll stay true to the boundary, especially if you meet someone you genuinely want to pursue. A boundary is a boundary, not a semipermeable membrane. Don't make exceptions. Don't let someone slip past your walls because they're especially hot. Remember why you made the boundary, and do your best to stay true to yourself rather than wavering for someone you recently met.

As you navigate new expectations and norms surrounding physical expectations, you should also begin to deconstruct Mormon assumptions about commitment. Mormons are commitment-obsessed. Conversations concerning marriage and family begin earlier than adolescence and prepare people to marry at eighteen, nineteen, and twenty. When I was eight, my mom lectured me on finding a returned-missionary spouse. I wrote heartfelt letters to my future husband during Young Women's lessons.

You may recognize in yourself a similar earnestness in dating, even after leaving the church. Single and dating Exmormons often share that they consciously and constantly think about marriage or long-term commitment with people they date casually. For most of the world, thinking about serious commitment early on is not pre-programmed. Mormons have an exceptional talent for thinking eternally, and relationships are no exception. Long-term planning is not necessarily negative but could lead to heartache and confusion when dating outside the church.

If you're picturing yourself married or living with every person you casually date, recognize where those thoughts originate. Early in the relationship, shift away from commitment and back to enjoying the person and getting to know them. Focus on companionship; focus on learning about who you are and who they are—stop thinking about eternity. Maybe you'll date this person once or twice, maybe for a year or a lifetime. Do not obsess over the future; allow yourself to enjoy the present.

Do not allow your relationship status to define your value as a human. Some married people are miserable. Some single people are supremely happy. Mormonism trains you to believe that single people aren't as successful or valuable. This is not true. Marriage and children are not the singular pinnacle of lifelong perfection. If you want these things in your life, do your best to find the person you want to spend your life with. But if you are still single, it doesn't mean you've failed the game of life. Focus on making yourself happy first. Live the version of your life that brings you the most joy and fulfillment. Do not wait for a relationship or marriage to find happiness.

In the church, men date actively, and women date passively. The man asks the woman, and the man pays for the date. Young women should always agree to the first date but never ask someone on a date themselves. As a woman leaving the church, you may have to take charge of your dating life more than you did in the church.

My friend Emily shared that she struggled to date after leaving the church. She didn't know how to approach other people. She was so used to men approaching her, asking her on dates, asking her on second dates, and on and on. If someone stopped texting her, she moved on. She was always pursued and never pursuing. Even when she met an amazing single person, she quietly hoped they would make the first move. She only wished they would approach or ask her out while doing nothing herself.

Emily resolved to take charge of her dating life. She realized she cared a lot more about finding the right person and actively pursuing them rather than hoping someone found her captivating enough to ask her out with zero prompting. If you're a single Exmormon woman, begin to put yourself out there and ask people on dates. Practice making the first move. When you meet someone interesting and exciting, ask for their number. Grab the reins of your life and pursue the people you want.

REFLECT AND WRITE

- How can you set and maintain boundaries in dating and sexual relationships? How can you communicate your desires with your partner or a potential partner?
- What specific hangups on sex and sexuality need to be addressed for you? How can you begin to work through the stigmas instilled by church teachings?
- What is the role of commitment and marriage in your life? Will you pursue marriage and a family, or is an alternative approach more enticing?
- How can you prioritize your sexual well-being, happiness, and self-acceptance out of the church?

MASTURBATION

Let's get one thing straight—masturbation is healthy. There is nothing sinful or dirty about it. If you feel guilty about masturbation, you can finally let that feeling float away along with your belief in The Book of Mormon. To admit something somewhat embarrassing, I did not masturbate till I was about twenty-eight. I was out of the church for several years before even attempting.

It was daunting, and I was too guilt-ridden and afraid to experiment as a teen or young adult. The church begins sexual shaming far before puberty. Recovering, even as an adult, is immensely difficult. Maybe you're like me, or perhaps masturbation has always been something you enjoyed but felt very guilty about.

Growing up, my genitals were very intimidating. I didn't want to look under the hood, much less touch or explore or even learn the names of the different parts of my body. Men are lucky because at least everything is on the outside, waiting to be observed and touched. Women aren't so fortunate. Everything is tucked away in a mostly out-of-sight area. It's taken me years to become comfortable learning about my body. That's pretty normal for most Mormons and even typical for irreligious people. Sex is taboo in and out of the church.

Once I got married, I realized I needed to figure out all my sexual hangups. I was barely willing to acknowledge my body. Having sex with another person was, to my surprise, not as straightforward as I thought it would be in my simple Mormon mind. To put it simply, if you don't know how to orgasm on your own, then asking someone else to figure out how to do it for you might not work either. Masturbation helps you take charge of your sexual experience.

Teaching masturbation is a sin is tantamount to teaching bodies and sexual organs themselves are sins. I've heard stories of Mormon men who avoid showering or keep a photo of Jesus in the shower to avoid the temptation to "sin." The church underwent a hyper-puritanical phase where *The Miracle of Forgiveness* was essentially doctrine. The echoes of this are still in the doctrine and remain lodged in the brains of anyone raised in Mormonism.

As Spencer W. Kimball shares in the book, "[Masturbation] too often leads to a grievous sin, even to that sin against nature, homosexuality. For, done in private, it evolves often into mutual masturbation—practiced with another person of the same sex—and thence into total homosexuality."

For a man who never masturbates, he certainly seems to know a lot about how it works and where it leads. I like to believe Spencer's information comes from personal experience. Jokes aside, masturbation is a healthy and safe sexual activity with many proven health benefits, like stress reduction and pain relief. It's a common myth that only men masturbate; women report masturbation in high numbers. And for the record, masturbation doesn't turn you gay. I don't think our species would have made it this far if it did.

Masturbation while in a relationship also doesn't mean your relationship is broken or something is wrong. If there is a desire discrepancy, this is a way for one party to experience sexual release without relying on or pressuring the other person. You are not responsible for your partner's sexual satisfaction and fulfillment; they are.

As you leave the church, embrace the opportunity to redefine your relationship with masturbation. Leave behind all the sexual shaming and begin to rewrite your relationship with your body. If possible, consider the benefits of masturbation on its own terms. Research the real risks and benefits rather than believing all the evil things taught by culture and the church.

If you are in a relationship, communicate about masturbation first. Discuss boundaries and how to masturbate while being respectful to the other person. This may be challenging since the church creates so much shame on the topic. If you're comfortable, suggest masturbating together or ask if they prefer to do it alone. Reread the communication process in Chapter Five for more tips.

If you have never masturbated before but want to try, a few simple steps are involved. Start in a setting where you are alone and do not need to worry about being interrupted. Wait for a time when you are relaxed and do not feel stressed.

Explore by gently touching and caressing sensitive areas of your body. Pay attention to how the different sensations feel. Explore whatever areas of the body are most responsive to sexual stimulation. Vary your technique and try circular, up and down, or side-to-side motions. Experiment with various levels of pressure. Try changing positions. Use sex toys. Some people, especially women, struggle to reach orgasm without sex toys. Build to an orgasm, or enjoy simple touching.

Men have an unambiguous indication of orgasm since it is almost always paired with ejaculation. For women, it is not so obvious. I've had conversations with adult women who have never had an orgasm before and are unclear what it feels like. Unfortunately, if you never masturbate, it may be challenging to climax with a partner. You are in your body and know what feels most intimately. For most people, if you want to learn how to orgasm, you must practice by yourself first.

For women, an orgasm is an intense pleasure. It is usually paired with muscle contractions of the pelvic floor muscles. These contractions can be more subtle or pronounced, depending on the individual. There is typically a feeling of release while the muscles are contracting. If you don't reach orgasm during every sexual encounter, you should not feel ashamed.

While you should not feel guilty, you should investigate why you didn't climax rather than accepting this as the reality for the rest of your sex life. Discuss sex openly, and be clear with your partner if your goal is to reach orgasm or if it is to enjoy closeness and touching.

Guilt and shame are difficult to overcome, and if you find yourself experiencing these emotions when masturbating or having sex, talk with a therapist. Feelings don't disappear; we can ignore them and shove them down, but ultimately, they will return—and will likely feel even worse. Do not think leaving the church will immediately eliminate years of sexual shame conditioning. Talk with your partner, a trusted friend, or a therapist if you are still experiencing these feelings.

PORNOGRAPHY

As Richard G. Scott said, "It is one of the most damning influences on earth." One might think he was speaking about opioids, child slavery, global warming, or racism. Nope—he's talking about pornography. Years of General Conference content would convince one there is no worse sin than watching porn. Each conference seems to have at least one talk on the topic, and the verbiage used to describe porn is dire, to say the least.

Some men in the church are forced to go to support groups which are the equivalent of "porn addict anonymous." Watching porn occasionally does not make you an addict. Looking at photos of naked girls does not mean you are evil. Most Mormon men who are "porn addicts" only watch porn a few times a week. They become so obsessively guilty about viewing porn; the shame makes the porn usage unbearable. After leaving the church, most men who were once "porn addicts" are miraculously cured. Not because they stop watching porn but because the religious guilt melts away.

When I watched pornography for the first time, I was shocked by its impact. Not because I became an immediate addict but because it seemed so benign compared to what I had pictured in my mind. In the same way I thought weed would destroy Jackson's life, I expected porn to incinerate mine. In the end, it was simply videos of naked people having sex. It was awkward and a little silly. Human connection is significantly more compelling than pixels moving across a screen.

If you experienced shame from a bishop because you watched porn, I hope you begin to let it go. You are still worthy of love. You still deserve to find a partner and get married (if that's what you want). You are still a good person. People who watch pornography are not disgusting. They are human. I am a mom with two kids, and I watch porn occasionally. I am still a good mom. I am still a good wife. My emotional bond with my spouse is deep-rooted.

To be fair, many people outside the church also take issue with pornography. The porn industry has many ethically challenging aspects. Much of porn is violent and sexist. It depicts sex, bodies, and relationships unrealistically. The overemphasis on men's orgasm and pleasure misrepresents balanced, healthy sex for some couples. Sex workers and adult film stars are often poorly treated, victimized, and dehumanized. Many people don't want their partner to watch pornography, which can be seen as infidelity.

However, the real issues associated with porn are not the issues the church keeps at the forefront. Porn is a sin. Porn is evil. Porn is damning. These words don't encourage a dialogue about the real and actual problems with porn. Instead, they induce shame and self-loathing in whoever sits through the conference talk. By a wide margin, most people—men and women—watch pornography at some point, and many people watch it regularly. Rather than shaming those who choose to watch pornography, it is wiser to educate yourself on the risks and moral implications.

If you choose to watch pornography, it is possible to watch ethically. Ethical porn is made with consent, performers and filmmakers are paid fairly for work, and everyone who participates is treated respectfully. Buying and watching content created and sold by an individual, or "amateur porn," ensures the person owns their image and consents to be filmed. Some videos include consent shared by the actors before the scene is shot. Research the companies producing the videos. Use websites known for creating ethical porn and companies that compensate performers well.

You can also use pornography to discover your sexual self. There are millions of different videos, each containing various combinations of people and sexual acts. Use the little black search bar to find something you like. You'll quickly discover some videos are erotic and attractive, while others disinterest you. This can help you learn about yourself, your likes, and your dislikes.

As an Exmormon, remember that many people will still find pornography immoral. If you are in a committed relationship, communicate with your partner. Mormon women are trained to feel like porn is incredibly threatening, and so expect hesitance and maybe even pushback from any hint of porn usage. If you worry this could lead to an argument, it may be best to bring this up in the context of couple's therapy.

In my experience, the people who are the most terrified of porn have never spent a single second of their lives viewing it. Porn is terrifying because they have absolutely no idea what pornography is, and they've been told to be afraid of it. I think everyone who leaves the church should watch a few videos. This isn't necessarily to use porn for sexual relief but to understand what pornography is and to defang it.

As a fresh Exmormon, reevaluate your relationship with pornography. If the thought of watching porn shoots feelings of impending doom through your body, ask why. Shame around sex, nudity, and sexual pleasure will probably remain with you, even after leaving. Whether or not you choose to watch porn should be informed by the risks and rewards, not by shame and self-loathing.

INVESTIGATING SEXUALITY

As summer slowly arrives and BYU graduation begins, I always look forward to the flurry of "coming out" posts on social media. Friends afraid of retaliation by the Honor Code Office wait in silence, keeping their sexuality a secret. Graduation and a diploma mark the long-awaited opportunity to come out without academic retribution.

Typically, these posts announce "I'm gay" and "I'm leaving the church" in a gorgeous gust of personal truth. Sadly, these young people have concealed themselves for so many years. I always feel immense happiness when my friends can finally live how they choose.

Questioning is the first step to discovering your sexuality. Many people are sure of what they want and who they are. Some gay, straight, and trans people have very early memories and experiences with identity.

Others who exit the church have repressed any sexual feelings contrary to the heterosexual Mormon norm, as Alex and Trace both shared in their stories. If you've silenced voices and desires year after year, you may be left unable to learn who you are and what you want. Sexuality and desire are a nuanced spectrum, and many people are not completely defined by one term or interest.

If you are already sure and confident of your sexual identity, this section may be less applicable.

If you are questioning, consider past crushes, including celebrities or fictional characters. What interested you, and why? There may be moments from the past that hinted at interest in something you didn't expect. Orientation can also change over time, or particular experiences may help direct you away from an early conclusion. You may feel compelled to give yourself a label and insert yourself into a box—it is better to accept that sexuality is fluid, and you can learn about yourself for an entire lifetime.

The most important aspect of questioning to center in your mind is self-compassion and allowing your brain to be a judgment-free zone. Research on Facebook or Reddit, and you will find Exmormon LGBTQIA+ groups to join. These spaces are almost always inclusive and provide a way to meet people with similar experiences and backgrounds. If you know someone queer, reach out and talk to them. Most queer people have gone down a similar road and will be able to help. They can help you understand yourself and can help you feel affirmed when you may feel otherwise.

Love yourself and know you are important, worthy, and good no matter your orientation. There is no differing value based on gender orientation or sexual expression between consenting adults. You have been conditioned to believe anything outside of heterosexuality is definitively evil. It's hard to get that voice out of your head.

SHARING SEXUALITY

Sharing your sexuality with your family and friends is entirely up to you. You do not owe anyone an explanation, though you may naturally want to give one to those you love. For those under eighteen or those still at a church-sponsored school, tread carefully. My heart goes out to anyone who wants to live with authenticity but is blocked by bigotry and homophobia. BYU banned queer relationships; for some, coming out to parents has led to homelessness.

This does not mean you and your identity are bad or wrong; your situation is bad and wrong. Don't let this keep you from being who you are inside—but be aware there may be consequences. You may choose to wait until you live by yourself to come out to specific people in your life; don't risk your safety when coming out.

If you want to share your sexuality with someone, start with the person who will be the most loving and accepting. This could be a close friend, a guidance counselor at school, or maybe a sibling. After you tell them, they can also be a sounding board for how to talk with other people in your life who may be less accepting. Be optimistic, but also emotionally prepare for pushback. Know there is nothing wrong with you; you are worthy and good. You are brave. If someone chooses not to accept you, it's their choice. It doesn't mean you are bad or wrong. Focus on loving and accepting yourself over worrying about what others will think.

Reach out for support from other members of the LGBTQIA+ community. Finding a support person can lift you when family members or teachings at church threaten to drag you down. When in doubt, give it time. There is no need to rush this process; be patient and go at your own pace.

My friend, Alexis Guel, grew up in the church and knew she was attracted to girls from a very young age. Her journey to acceptance was long and complicated. Her story is powerful and adds significant insight into what it means to investigate and accept sexuality after leaving Mormonism.

ALEX'S STORY

There were butterflies when I saw her; there wasn't any mistaking it. I was nine when I felt that awkward, shy, and embarrassed tinge you feel when you have a crush but are too young to know what to do about it. I knew it early on. My thoughts of shamelessly falling in love with some of my friends confirmed it for me. I was queer.

But I was taught the entire thing was wrong. Those feelings, though they felt true, weren't true. I prayed and cried, pleading to know why I was made a woman and why I was made to feel this way. It was forced into my mind over and over and over again by leaders, members, and others I looked up to in the Mormon church that this isn't how I should live my life. Horror stories of endless unhappiness were ingrained in my mind. People like me deserved the worst - sexual abuse, abandonment, and a life without love. I needed a safe option, a place where choice was taken from me. I went to BYU.

There would be no way I could express my feelings in an institution with such oppressive rules. However, I constantly yearned to live my truth; it all weighed on me, and I became suicidal. The constant pressure everywhere to marry, fit into a cookie-cutter mold, and be who everyone else was unbearable. But I did what I was told: I quickly started dating a returned missionary. On my twentieth birthday, I found myself engaged and, six weeks later, married.

Over the years, the feelings never went away. Sometimes, I would daydream of escaping or being "saved," as if I were in some terrible situation that I needed rescuing from. I ached for more and couldn't will myself to be happy. Countless nights, I sobbed myself to sleep next to my husband. I couldn't make it stop and was confused as to why I couldn't shut the thoughts in my head far away.

Why couldn't I be happy? I hated myself for it at first, but I grew to forgive myself. It wasn't my fault—this is who I am. And conforming to an arbitrary "one size fits all" plan wouldn't help me. I removed my name from the records at twenty-three and took control of my life. I began to stand up for myself, I started loving my body, and I began to listen to myself more closely than ever before

At twenty-five, I made the hard decision to continue that and file for divorce. Divorce is an awful thing I don't wish on anyone. It hurts and stings for years to come. However, I finally, for the first time in my life, felt truly free. The eating disorder I had since I was thirteen suddenly stopped. I started dating women and felt comfortable enough to experiment and use toys in the bedroom. I became incredibly in tune with my body and emotions. It was as if I was asleep the entire time and suddenly woke up.

This was my first time dating outside of the church. At times, it was scary—I recall the first STD test I ever took. I was alone in the cold doctor's office, waiting for someone to take a sample of my urine and blood. I was twenty-five, and this was my first time in this office. When I looked around the waiting room, there were people younger and older than me: people who had been living their life freely for years. Then there I was—like a baby.

When I left Mormonism, I missed the community. When I embraced my sexuality, I suddenly found the same sense of community. It was beautiful—people who loved and accepted you regardless of your past or identity. They loved you because you just were. That was something not even the church gave me.

Although it was difficult, I am grateful to be where I am today. I wish I could go back in time and tell myself to embrace myself sooner. At first, I hated myself for it—I felt ridiculous for letting so much time pass without actually being myself. My precious early twenties were spent wearing garments and avoiding sex toys. Then I forgave myself. I am who I am because of my past. I love myself for that, and my partner does too.

WORK IN PROGRESS

I'm thrilled to announce that Britney Spears is part of my regular rotation of favorite music. She sings, "If You Seek Amy," into my ears as I run or do dishes. However, I turn down the volume if other people are around. I love wearing bikinis. But sometimes, I slip into the water as quickly as possible to avoid people seeing so much of my skin. Masturbation and pornography no longer scare me, though admitting I participate in these activities—even to a Google doc—makes me blush.

This was the most daunting chapter to write because sex and sexuality are still my biggest hangups as an Exmormon. Even after leaving the church, I could barely discuss sex with Jackson. It took me years of practice to ask for what I wanted. My body still intimidates me sometimes. Each time I take a few steps forward, I take at least one back.

Maybe by the time I am forty or fifty, I'll be ready to embrace sex and sexuality with complete excitement and without shame. Experimenting with drugs and trying cocktails for the first time was thrilling. Getting over my sexual shame has been a daunting uphill battle. The church still has its claws deep in my brain. On top of Mormon shame, sex is taboo in mainstream American culture. None of us are exactly set up for success on this topic.

Sex still intimidates me. Even talking about certain aspects of sex scares me. But every time I conquer a mental block, I feel ecstatically proud of myself. Sex should be one of the most beautiful, wonderful, and fun aspects of human existence. The church robbed me of this, and now it's my responsibility to steal it back for myself.

You deserve to love sex. You deserve to love and explore your body without any shame or embarrassment. You deserve good sex that helps you feel close to your chosen person. You deserve to love whoever you choose, regardless of orientation or gender. If these truths aren't true for you, take your first step. Conquer this mountain in your mind. Shut Mormon shame out with iron bars. You can do this. I can do this. Let's work on it together.

NINE
CIVICS
Political Paradigm Shift

The arc of the moral universe is long,
but it bends torward justice.

—Martin Luther King Jr.

"I guess it's fine if people are gay—I just don't think they should be able to get married," I said smoothly, looking across the couch at Jackson.

We sat in an apartment a quick walk from the J. Reuben Clark Law School on the BYU campus. If I had stopped someone strolling past the stairs of the brick building and shared the same sentiment, I would have likely heard a quick and absolute assent.

The look in Jackson's eye was foreign to me, a mix of surprise and dismay. We had been dating for a month, and his reaction caught me off guard. Here in this room, I assumed I was safe sharing this viewpoint. I wouldn't have said this to friends in high school or coworkers from my hometown. But here, in an apartment at the base of Y Mountain, I expected to vocalize this bigoted opinion without dispute. I could casually espouse a belief I heard from religious leaders, my parents, and BYU professors.

After a brief pause, Jackson asked, "But why should other people have to live according to your religious beliefs?"

My stomach dropped, and I began to trip over my words, thinly arguing my position. "Well, I guess... marriage should be between a man and a woman. That's what marriage is."

He pushed, "I think marriage is a legal contract between two consenting adults. A man and a man can marry, live together, and be happy. How does that impact you? If they are not harming anyone, why should there be a law to keep them from living in the way they choose? Why should the right to marry be legally stripped from them?"

I stared at him blankly. "I'm confused. You're Mormon, and you served a mission. Why are you disagreeing with me?"

Driving home that night, my mind raced. *Should I break up with him?* I wondered, *No good Mormon is okay with gay marriage.*

Jackson was never a perfect Peter Priesthood. He smoked in high school. He skipped college and opted to get a job as soon as he returned from his mission. He also played Dungeons and Dragons. When I shared this with my mom, she asked if he could be a good father. And on top of all that, Jackson often disagreed with many Mormon political beliefs.

So many of his views and life experiences weren't textbook Mormonism. It was off-putting and enticing all at once. At BYU, every first date felt like one caricature after the other. Always the same conversations, the same ideas, and the same person with a slightly different face—over and over again.

After our gay marriage conversation, I realized I was a caricature, too. My casual disavowal of gay rights revealed how easily I expected to fall into the same worn-out conversation. My beliefs were unexamined, and I couldn't defend my position because I was only squawking like a parrot. When I said, "Gay marriage bad," I assumed I would hear "Gay marriage bad," affirmed in return.

Mormonism and Republicanism go together like cheese and macaroni. Though messages from the pulpit are not usually overtly political, Mormons often have strong political convictions. This caused a bit of a stir during the pandemic when President Nelson encouraged members to wear masks, and many still didn't. Republicans tend to be anti-immigration, though the church generally seems to favor open borders. Globally, the church is a fairly neutral political force, but within the corners of Utah, it reigns supreme. From laws on conversion therapy to state liquor laws, the church runs a quasi-theocracy.

I graduated from high school with a clear view of how a good Mormon votes. The most critical issues are socially conservative, like restricting access to abortion and same-sex marriage. The government's role should be to regulate people's actions in day-to-day life. Social smut, like drinking in the open or pornography, should be illegal. Mormons love capitalism and believe there should be little federal oversight in the financial sector. This may be why seemingly every Mormon bishop is rich, and the church wholeheartedly protects and enjoys its tax-free status.

Exiting the church means confronting and negotiating the countless parts of yourself entangled with your past religion. I am still navigating this myself, and my purpose for writing this chapter is not to tell you what to believe politically. The Mormon-trained mind hungers after certain truth and testimony. It is disillusioning to realize the world is full of nuance and shades of gray.

Cognitive dissonance keeps us safe, and it stunts growth. Recoiling from new information is easier than changing our thoughts, actions, and sometimes entire lives. I find significantly more value in the strength to say, "I am still learning," and "I am not sure yet." Conversations are much more exciting when both parties are willing to learn from each other instead of entrenching themselves more and more deeply into the perspectives each brings to the table.

I can't provide the answer to every question, and you should be very skeptical of anyone who says they can. Anyone who declares themselves the fountain of knowledge usually concludes by asking for some type of political donation—or ten percent of your income. Instead of searching for a new prophet to follow, develop a practice for evaluating your beliefs. Search for ways to challenge existing assumptions and change your mind when confronted with new information. Embrace saying, "I don't know."

Recognize this is an inherently emotional process. Changing your mind can be physically painful. Recall the first time you read the CES Letter or watched a YouTube video about early church history. You probably stopped halfway through because it was too much to handle. Words like "earth-shattering" get thrown around because these moments can make you feel as if your brain is splitting into ribbons.

Be patient and accept that you may not be ready to navigate some beliefs for a few months or even years. After my conversation with Jackson about gay marriage and some extensive reading on the topic, I changed my mind in a few weeks. A few months later, in 2015, the church unveiled a rule prohibiting children of gay parents from being baptized before their eighteenth birthday. This new policy was a huge catalyst propelling my exit from the church.

My stance on gay marriage transformed in a few months. Meanwhile, my point of view on abortion is still developing and changing. I'm at peace with this reality. I've spent enough of my life standing at a pulpit saying, "I know," over and over and over again.

Below is my framework for re-evaluating beliefs, along with a few examples of how to use it to assess common political positions. At each step, take a deep breath. When and if you feel some brain burn, picture your exhausted muscles at the end of a long workout. Stretch your mind into places it has never adventured.

While this chapter uses the framework for political beliefs, you can use it for any perspective or understanding you want to examine more closely.

FRAMEWORK FOR RE-EVALUATING BELIEFS

1. **Write the original belief down.**
   - Jot down your belief. Express it as clearly as possible.
   - Include any assumptions* that support the belief.
   - Put your notebook aside to refer back to later.

2. **Challenge the belief and assumptions with research and study.**
   - Find books, articles, and videos on the topic. Search for resources that disagree or conflict with your position, and don't get all your information from the same source or person. If you Google "Reasons why X is bad," make sure to search for "Reasons why X is good."
   - Find commentators from across the spectrum of belief. This could be podcasters, politicians, YouTubers, writers, or scholars. Search for people who speak and think differently than you do. Find people from different backgrounds, countries, social classes, and time periods. The goal is not to find some new, all-knowing person but to practice listening to differing perspectives on an ongoing basis. If some stance bothers you, figure out why.
   - Talk to real people. Find someone in your circle who you trust and speak with them candidly. An echo chamber is when everyone agrees with you, and there is no opportunity or invitation for debate (think Sunday School). On Twitter, you'll find the opposite: millions of deeply entrenched perspectives. Search for sincere conversation—look for a thought partner to challenge you without arguing.

3. **Ask: Does this belief still fit in my value system?**
   - Be willing to admit a belief you hold is wrong or needs to be altered in some way. Sift through the different aspects of your belief and analyze which portions still resonate and hold up under scrutiny. Let go of "being sure."
   - Accept that change will always be more complex and more painful than staying the same. If conversations often end in arguments or hurt feelings, you may not be ready to confront and renegotiate this belief.

4. **Read your initial statement out loud and rewrite as needed.**
   - As you reread, compare it with your new notes. Consider the conversations you've had and the research you've completed. Do you still feel the same, or have you changed? Highlight the portions you need to change. This may be a few words, or you may highlight every single word.
   - After deciding what needs to change, write the new version of your belief beneath your original take. Rewrite it completely or combine the new with the old to create an up-to-date statement.

5. **Repeat the process over and over again.**
   - Your mind is a changing organism, and new experiences and information will and should alter your point of view. Keeping a record of beliefs is a fantastic way to watch this metamorphosis over time.

*An assumption is something accepted as accurate or as sure to happen without proof. A typical American assumption is "all people are equal" and "anyone can pull themselves up with their bootstraps." However, as you walk around your city, you'll observe both homelessness and extreme wealth on the same street.

Every culture is full of assumptions. A commonly held Mormon assumption is "a mother should spend as much time with her children as possible" and "a man's first responsibility is financially providing for the family." Beliefs are often founded on assumptions that may not hold much water under scrutiny. Some women flourish as working parents, while some men are excellent stay-at-home parents.

USING THE FRAMEWORK: GAY MARRIAGE

Below is an illustration of using the framework topically to examine gay marriage. While reading my example, consider which topics you want to put under scrutiny. In my initial description of my belief, I wrote down many arguments against gay marriage I've heard from Mormons over the years, many of which are positions I used to hold myself. This is not to say all active Mormons feel this way; it is just an illustration of a commonly held cultural belief and a way to use the framework to examine the belief.

Write the original belief down, then challenge the belief and assumptions.

Belief: Marriage is between a man and a woman. Same-sex marriage should not be legal.

• • •

Assumption: Gay marriage is morally wrong and bad for society, and being gay is a sin. The United States is a Christian nation that should exist according to Christian values.

Challenge: One religion should not dictate how every person lives. The United States is not a Christian nation, and the First Amendment to the Constitution states everyone in the United States has the right to practice their religion or no religion at all. There should be a clear separation between church and state to maintain the rights of all people, regardless of belief. Gay marriage does no clear, systematic, or measurable harm to society or any individual.

• • •

Assumption: Gay marriage is morally wrong and bad for society, and being gay is a sin. The United States is a Christian nation that should exist according to Christian values.

Challenge: One religion should not dictate how every person lives. The United States is not a Christian nation, and the First Amendment to the Constitution states everyone in the United States has the right to practice their religion or no religion at all. There should be a clear separation between church and state to maintain the rights of all people, regardless of belief. Gay marriage does no systematic, or measurable harm to society or individuals.

• • •

Assumption: Gay marriages do not contribute to society in the same way heterosexual marriages do.

Challenge: Gay people have jobs, hold political office, and participate in their communities. They own and maintain homes, pay taxes, and donate to nonprofits. If straight people are unemployed or alcoholics, they are not legally held from civil marriage. When straight celebrities are married for a few months, then divorce, it is still considered a marriage both socially and legally. Societal worthiness or contribution has nothing to do with a marriage between two people.

• • •

Assumption: Marriage is a religious institution, and gay marriage is not aligned with Christian belief.

Challenge: Marriage is a religious institution, and it is also a civil institution. There are many advantages associated with a legal marriage, like hospital visitation, asset protection, health care access, and tax benefits. The legal and societal benefits of marriage indicate this union should be available to all consenting adults, not just adults who believe and participate in Christianity.

• • •

Assumption: Gay people cannot procreate and can't have normal, nuclear families. Marriage is for creating families and having children.

Challenge: When heterosexual individuals cannot procreate, they are not legally barred from marriage. If a heterosexual person is charged with child abuse or becomes a felon, the law does not restrict him from having another child. Parental worthiness or ability has no legal power to keep someone from marriage.

Add some research and study.

Book List

- *Queer: A Graphic History* by Dr. Meg-John Barker and Julia Scheele
- *Stand by Me: The Forgotten History of Gay Liberation* by Jim Downs
- *Am I Blue? Coming Out from the Silence* by Marion Dane Bauer

Podcast List

- Latter-Gay Stories
- Latter-Day Lesbian
- Peace Out

List of friends to talk with

- William
- Olivia
- Ben
- Henry

Ask: Does this belief still fit in my value system?

> Nope, it's time to change my position.

Rewrite the new belief.

> **New Belief:** Gay people have as much right to marriage as straight people. Marriage should be available legally for consenting adults.
>
> **Supports:** All people deserve the love, happiness, and legal protections found in marriage, regardless of sexuality, gender orientation, or expression.
>
> Marriage is a civil agreement between two people, and there are many benefits found within marriage. These advantages should be available to everyone.
>
> Being gay holds just as much value and morality as being straight. It is not inferior, and it is not a sin. Gay people deserve a place in society and in their communities like anyone else.
>
> Religious people can practice their beliefs, and gay people can get married. The two are not mutually exclusive. One person's beliefs must not infringe on the other person's rights.

Repeat the process over and over again.

USING THE FRAMEWORK: ABORTION

A primary reason Millennials and Gen Z leave the church is gay marriage and LGBTQ+ treatment. Americans broadly support gay marriage, and when individuals leave the church, they typically adopt the consensus opinion on gay marriage. As soon as I stopped believing in Mormonism, I fervently supported LGBTQ+ protections and rights.

I used the framework for gay marriage to illustrate what I consider as an "easier" position for most people. It is easier because when you support gay marriage, you align with the general public. This is also the case for alcohol consumption, tank-top wearing, and living with someone before you marry them. These positions are easy to adopt because they feel "normal" compared to Mormon idealism.

Some beliefs are not so simple to rewrite. After I left the church, I struggled to reassess my feelings surrounding abortion. I registered as a Democrat after I left the church and spent time reading and consuming media about abortion. After Roe V. Wade was overturned, I saw an image of a woman protesting at the Supreme Court. Her large, swollen belly was covered in the words, "NOT YET A HUMAN." She had to be in her third trimester. The image made my insides squirm in the most unexpected way.

As we drive to Dallas from Austin, we cross billboard after billboard with photos of adorable, blue-eyed babies. Each sign is splashed with statements like, "Life begins at conception" and "Heartbeat at six weeks." I picture the ten-year-old in Ohio who had to cross state lines to receive an abortion after a twenty-seven-year-old man raped her. I imagine the Texas woman who nearly died from infection after she was denied an abortion to remove a miscarriage.

As these images swirl through my mind, I look in the rearview mirror at my two young sons. My heart pulls me in half, one side pulling towards the rights of the children and the other pushing closer to the rights of women. Each side appears at odds. I've spoken with some who say a woman should have the right to have an abortion at any time and for any reason, even at the fortieth week of pregnancy. Others say "the morning after" pill is equal to murder.

As I weigh these two halves, I ardently feel a sense that there *is* a correct answer. My heart yearns for the safety of knowing. The decisiveness on either side unbalances me. I'm reminded of all those hours spent in fasting and testimony meetings, hearing people declare they know exactly what happens when we die without a shadow of a doubt.

When it comes to abortion, I still reside in the messy middle of indecision. My emotions and opinions whirl around my brain, changing and morphing bit by bit as I consume some new information. I want to illustrate using the framework when your opinion is still crystalizing, as mine is.

Write the original belief down.

Belief: Abortion is murder. Women should not have the right to kill another human living inside them. Once you're pregnant, you should not have the choice to end the pregnancy.

• • •

Assumption: Life begins at conception. Once the sperm reaches the egg, the baby inside the womb is just as human as anyone walking on the street. When an abortion is performed, a human life is taken.

Challenge: When an egg is fertilized, it is clearly not yet a baby. After fertilization, the organism is a clump of dividing cells that could not survive outside the womb. These cells form into a tiny embryo. By the eleventh week, the embryo becomes a fetus. There is no definitive line between "not human" to "human."

Nearly 99 percent of abortions occur before 21 weeks. When abortion is needed later in pregnancy, it's often in highly complex circumstances. Usually, an abortion is performed after 21 weeks because the baby's heartbeat has ceased, and an abortion is performed to remove the dead infant. If the body is not removed, there is significant risk of infection. Medical treatment for nonviable pregnancies, like an ectopic pregnancy, is typically the same as an abortion.

• • •

Assumption: Human life is sacred. Legal abortion promotes a culture where life is disposable.

Challenge: Human life *is* sacred, which means an unborn child's life *and* the mother's life are both sacred. Women deserve access to quality pre and postnatal care if human life is sacred. The US has the worst postpartum leave—meaning no guaranteed leave at all—of any developed country. As a society, we should value human life at every stage, not just unborn fetuses. If a woman or child has been raped or is the victim of incest, they should not be forced to carry a baby.

American culture and law treat some human life as "more disposable" than others. Notice the difference in news coverage when an indigenous woman goes missing verses when an upper-middle-class white woman disappears. Note the benefits provided to a CEO versus those provided to a migrant farmer.

Everyone is very obviously not equal in our country. Many people need us to take the mantra "human life is sacred" more seriously, like those experiencing homelessness and refugees.

• • •

Assumption: Women should not be able to choose to end a life. The unborn child's life trumps the woman's choice over what to do with her body.

Challenge: Women typically don't want accidental pregnancies. Pregnancy is dangerous, and childrearing is tremendously difficult. Women who give birth to unexpected pregnancies are much more likely to experience extreme poverty, impacting the child and any children the woman may already have.

When women have access to early-term abortion, they can terminate a pregnancy before the fetus becomes viable. When a fetus is not yet viable, women should be able to choose for themselves rather than being forced, by law, to carry a pregnancy.

• • •

Assumption: Women should carry the baby for nine months and give it up for adoption if they don't want to raise it themselves.

Challenge: This callous analysis of a woman's relationship with her children completely discounts a mother's feelings. Statistically, most women who consider an abortion but don't get one end up keeping the baby. A week after being denied an abortion, only 14% of the women said they were considering putting the baby up for adoption. There is a marked difference between aborting at ten weeks versus giving away a newborn child.

Women who want an abortion are not trying to use a "get out of jail free card." Women pursue abortion because they know they cannot support a child. If they keep the child, they will be more likely to experience poverty and a myriad of other trials. The child will experience these things as well. However, after a baby carried to term is born, it is exceedingly difficult for women to simply give the baby away.

Add some research and study.

Book List

- *Abortion in America: The Origins and Evolution of National Policy* by James C. Mohr

- *Defenders of the Unborn: The Pro-Life Movement Before Roe v. Wade* by Daniel K. Williams
- *What It Means to Be Human: The Case for the Body in Public Bioethics* by O. Carter Snead

Podcast List

- Banned by NPR
- Access: A Podcast About Abortion
- No Body Criminalized

List of friends to talk with

- Sophia
- Emma
- Mia

Ask: Does this belief still fit in my value system?

Nope, it's time to change my position.

Rewrite the new belief.

New Belief: Abortion is an incredibly complex issue. The availability of abortion should be based on the progression of the fetus, the mother's health, and the pregnancy's circumstances.

Supports: Women deserve access to better resources and support surrounding childbirth and childrearing. There would be fewer abortions if women could adequately care for a pregnancy and the resulting child.

Third-trimester abortion should only be available in extreme cases. Past twenty-one weeks, I believe most abortions should be restricted. Abortions should be available to anyone seeking one before this time.

> We need to trust women to make the best decisions for their lives and circumstances. Laws mandating women carry unwanted pregnancies starting at six weeks are cruel and overreaching. Women are not irresponsible murderers. Women deserve body autonomy and freedom to choose what is best for their families.

Repeat the process over and over again.

As you read through my abortion analysis, you may have thought, "These arguments aren't very well developed," or "These viewpoints are paradoxical." You are right. I feel it in myself even as I write it on the page. That is the point. I assume I will never be able to write out an incredibly compelling rationale for abortion. You can feel the indecision waving like a flag during a hurricane.

Let it be exciting instead of disappointing. It's okay not to know exactly how you feel, even on such a vital topic as abortion. Maybe in a few years, I'll finally land in a definitive position, and I'll rewrite my belief on the topic for one final time. I am not there yet. And that's okay.

On the following page is a list of common political concepts with unique ties to Mormonism and conservatism. These are topics I often heard my parents discussing or that I discussed with my friends in my ward. Not all Mormons have the same political beliefs. The list is generalized and not meant to depict every Mormon.

As you review the list, choose one or two topics to use with the framework. If you use the framework to reassess a political belief, choose something still in development. Challenge yourself to confront and renegotiate the most complex issues.

COMMON POLITICAL BELIEFS WITHIN MORMONISM

- Gay marriage should be illegal.
- Evolution discounts the existence of God and should not be taught in schools.
- Drugs should be illegal, and there should be heavy penalties for anyone buying, selling, or using drugs.
- Racism is no longer a significant issue in our country. Great progress has been made on race relations, so we don't need to address it often.
- The United States of America is the greatest nation on earth. Policies should always prioritize USA interests and values.
- The United States is fundamentally Christian, and God should be present in government.
- Gender roles are vital to society and should be honored, upheld, and protected.
- Climate change is a mostly made-up problem.
- Gun ownership is an American right. There should be very few, if any, restrictions around gun ownership.
- Religious freedom should be protected at all costs. Laws that permit immoral activities like gay marriage threaten religious freedom. Churches deserve tax-exempt status.
- Welfare and social programs only disable people further and teach them to depend on the government.
- Schools should teach abstinence-only sex education. Books about sex and sexuality should be kept out of schools.

REFLECT AND WRITE

- Think of a conversation where your beliefs were challenged. How did you respond, and did your beliefs change as a result?
- Consider the list of common political beliefs within Mormonism. Are there any of these beliefs that you've held or still hold? How have your views on these topics evolved as you've left the church, if at all?
- Think about a situation where you've encountered cognitive dissonance, where your beliefs conflicted with new information. How did you handle it, and what did you learn from the experience?
- Use the "Framework for Re-evaluating Beliefs" outlined on page 210 to analyze one of your current beliefs or convictions. Take a belief, write it down, list its assumptions, challenge it with research, and reflect on whether it still fits within your value system.
- Think of a time you felt pressured to conform to certain beliefs or political views due to your social or cultural environment. How did you handle this pressure, and did it lead to personal growth or internal conflict?

CIVIC ACTIVITY AND YOUR NEWFOUND BELIEFS

The Mormon missionary urge is strong. As a missionary, my beliefs motivated me to work from dawn to dusk, knocking on doors and talking to people in Target aisles. The desire to change the world and evangelize for a cause doesn't go away, even after leaving the church.

As you land on new positions and political beliefs, you will likely need to share your opinions. Belief and action fall hand in hand, and you can share and act on your new beliefs in countless ways. The easiest way is to vote. Casting a ballot is a simple and powerful way to speak out for your new beliefs.

Rather than voting along party lines, learn about candidates and their positions. Maybe you're a Republican; perhaps you're a Democrat. Neither party gets everything right, and it's easy to find representatives on either side who didn't uphold campaign promises to constituents. Search for candidates and elected officials who you actually believe in.

Attending political rallies and protests is another way to participate within your community and take a stand for a particular belief. Choose an unformulated belief and choose an event to attend. Writing this chapter made me want to attend a march or rally focused on abortion. Talking with people is a great way to continue to develop your beliefs on an issue.

There are many other ways to get involved in the community and to speak out for your beliefs. Volunteer with a great organization, donate to a nonprofit, or start a new movement. Sharing articles or writing a thoughtful post on social media is also a meaningful way to impact your social circle. Voicing an unpopular opinion may be scary, but it often gives others permission to be open, too.

ON THE EQUALITY OF WOMEN AND MEN

I want you to open Google on your phone and type "LDS church leadership" into the search bar. Go to the images tab and find the General Authority and Officers chart. While I'm sure most active Mormons have seen this chart before, look at it through a new lens this time. This chart is a wall of happy, smiling (mostly) white men staring back at you.

Sure, there are a few photos of women smushed to the side. This change happened in 2015 when the church appointed women to executive councils for the first time. Sure, women are given "leadership positions" in the church—leadership in Primary, Young Women, and Relief Society. These women are in charge of other women and girls. No matter how high or low you look in the church, you'll never find a woman with the authority to make choices for a man's life.

Think of what it does to girls and boys when they grow up looking at a chart like this. I include boys because girls *and* boys are both impacted by seeing power take one specific form, day to day. When you grow up seeing this representation of power, you quickly conclude what type of people matter most. When you walk into church on Sunday, the conclusions are confirmed. The bishop and his counselors sit up on the podium, watching over the flock. Typically, the only woman on the podium is the pianist.

Even as a little girl, I knew men were more important than women. And though you might expect a girl to rebel against this unfair power structure, my mind turned me the other way. I also thought women were weak. My dad constantly used the phrase, "You X, Y, and Z like a girl." Any time I revealed any weakness associated with womanhood, I was ridiculed. In reaction, I attempted to crush any impulse toward femininity.

But try as I might, I always was just still a girl. My destiny would always be motherhood. I was told to get a degree "In case your future husband dies." Growing up in the church, I was constantly told my clothing didn't cover me enough. Even if clothing went past my knees and to my elbows, it was somehow still "form fitting."

As I searched through the scriptures, I rarely saw the names of women. When women did appear in scripture, it was always in some association with men. The only thing a woman learned about her purpose in life is to be a better wife or mother. Even Esther, arguably the most prominent and influential woman in the Bible, is chosen by the king because she is *beautiful*. From gender roles to polygamy to temple ceremonies, the Mormon church is an inherently sexist, patriarchal tradition.

These teachings and representations lead most girls and boys to the same conclusion: men are more important than women. This teaching is rarely said aloud but is depicted and demonstrated everywhere. If men are more important than women, it means their thoughts, opinions, and lives do not matter as much as men. It means women are subhuman.

If men are more important than women, should a woman have the power to choose what happens in her life? What can a woman know, anyway? She should look to a man to tell her how to spend money, when and if to seek education, and when to reproduce. In a tradition where men matter more than women, women will never have genuine autonomy. She cannot know for herself better than what a man can know. What's more, she may not even believe she deserves freedom or autonomy if she comes of age in a sexist, patriarchal religion like Mormonism.

For a long time, I thought about all these things about women. When boys and men see men in power, most believe that men matter more than women. It also means women think men are more important than women. Growing up in the church infused me with my own version of toxic masculinity.

A few years after leaving the church, I carried a heavy tray full of food for a work event. While prepping the food for the event, I saw men struggle to bring these trays out of the kitchen. When I finished preparing the food, I picked up one of the large trays to help move them into the event space.

I was a few months pregnant at the time, but I resolved to do my part and brought the tray down the hall. As I carried it out of the cafeteria and into the event space, several people stopped and asked to take the tray. I refused every time. Finally, after a few minutes of walking, I reached the table and set down the tray.

Beads of sweat had formed over my forehead and back, and I was panting. As I sat down to rest, I rested my hand over my stomach. I felt a little queasy, like I might throw up. *Why didn't I accept the help when it was offered?* I wondered, surprised by my refusal. The people around me had kindly offered to help, and I had outrightly rejected them.

Because accepting help makes me just another weak woman, I thought. In that moment, I realized that even though I had left the church years ago, I still had a significant amount of internalized sexism. I still hated parts of myself because I still considered women less than men. Accepting help was tantamount to admitting I was less valuable than a man.

Even though I had tried coffee and no longer thought drinking beer would turn me into the devil, this was a pernicious piece of the church that remained anchored in my mind and heart. I still found myself falling into patterns of rejecting femininity and replacing it with as much masculinity as possible. As long as I could be masculine, I could be a little more important.

In that moment I realized that even though I had left the church years ago, I still had a significant amount of internalized sexism. Men and women can be sexist. I still have small levels of toxic masculinity coursing through me. Little girls *and* little boys are impacted by the message that only men matter. And men don't matter either unless they are willing to act in a very specific, masculine manner.

Femininity isn't inherently bad. Masculinity isn't inherently bad. Society transforms these two ways of acting and being into "bad" when it ascribes value to one over the other. When one way of being is more valuable than another, it means one has power over the other.

When and if you find yourself assuming men are better than women, recognize where that thought originates. Everything from the church to our broader society has messaged this throughout your life. All top LDS church leaders are men. Most CEOs are men. Most of the world's wealthiest people are men. Watch any of the most popular movies from before 2010, and you'll rarely see a woman. If you do see a woman, she'll be talking about a man.

With this societal track record, it's not surprising that men and women are at odds regarding power. When little boys grow up seeing only men in power and only men speaking, they may begin to believe only men should be at the mic and hold leadership positions. It's not a surprising conclusion to draw. But now it's our responsibility to dismantle it.

Men are not more important than women. Deconstructing this messaging takes a long time, and I am still working on it.

I love being a mother, but I have to remind myself continuously that being a mother doesn't make me less important as a member of society. Being a mother doesn't mean that is all I am. And just because I am a mother doesn't mean I don't deserve a powerful voice in my community and my family.

Recognize and acknowledge your biases. The Mormon church creates significant biases concerning gender. Begin to educate yourself on the history and impact of sexism. Discuss the experience of being a man or woman with the people around you. You may be surprised to learn what it is like to grow up in the church as a little boy or girl. What is the impact of being told: "Boys don't cry." What is the impact of being told: "You only need a degree if your husband dies."

Challenge stereotypes. Consider your existing beliefs on how men and women act. Look around your life, in the media, and in the news for examples of men and women confronting stereotypes. Examine your language and behavior. Consider words and phrases you might use that are sexist. Even an innocuous phrase like, "You're not like the other girls," might sound like a compliment, but it's actually putting down all other women.

Support women in leadership and the workplace. When you see sexism, say something. Use the influence you have to support women in their roles and help them to be successful. Be respectful and treat everyone with dignity and respect. The reason women are not in leadership roles as often as men is not because they are not able, but because they have been kept from the board room.

You've left the church behind. Now, leave the sexism and misogyny behind, too. And, as I've tried to make clear, this section is for men *and* women. The sexist messaging of the church negatively impacts men *and* women. Marriages can never thrive if one party is more powerful. It sets us up for failure in our relationships and our workplaces. Gender inequality is a moral evil; though we did not create it, it's our job to stop it.

Next time a man offers to help me carry something very heavy, I plan on saying, "Yes, thank you! It is kind of you to offer." And next time a man catcalls me while I'm strolling down the sidewalk, I plan on shouting "Fuck you!" in response. I love being a mother, and I love investing in the S&P. French braiding hair and killing massive spiders both come to me quite easily. I'm handy with a drill. I cry at the smallest things.

I am not a one-dimensional cartoon, and neither are you. Every person you meet is a complex organism with a beating heart and a one-of-a-kind mind. Let's pause and look at each other more deeply rather than relying on stereotypes, biases, and clichés.

TEN

COMMENCEMENT

Becoming an Ex-Exmormon

And now that you don't have to be perfect, you can be good.

—John Steinbeck

One morning in June, I stepped out for a run. The hazy morning was muggy, and the temperature pushed above 95 degrees. After a few miles, I took my shirt off and began to run in a sports bra.

It was my pink sports bra, the one I usually avoid wearing because, at certain angles, my nipples show. I was behind on laundry, so it was the only sports bra left in my drawer that morning. Hunching over a bit, I continued my pace. The breeze spiraled past my stomach, and I felt a bit of cool relief.

Running up to the gates of my apartment complex, I looked down at my phone to stop my running app and answer a text.

For a moment, my mind was lost in my phone. Tires on gravel sounded quietly behind me.

"Excuse me, miss?"

I turned around. A younger man was sitting in a white car twenty-five feet away. He was looking at me. His teeth shined as he smiled out at me. The oversized, dark sunglasses he wore flashed when he turned his head.

"Can you help me with directions? I'm looking for..." his voice trailed off abruptly, and I took a few steps closer.

"Excuse me?" I asked, returning his smile politely.

"I'm trying to find the Woods Apartments."

"What? There's nothing around here with that name."

The man mumbled again; it sounded like another question. I walked forward one more time, straining to figure out what he was saying. He stretched back against the leather seat of the car and moved his arms away from his lap. Very suddenly, the world churned and turned red.

His pants were unzipped, and he was masturbating.

My stomach dropped, and for a split second, I became ice. Eyes flicking back to his face, I saw the plastic smile replaced with a vile sneer.

"FUCKYOUFUCKYOUFUCKYOU," I screamed, running at the car.

There was no plan, only anger. The car peeled away from me. I ran after it for five or six steps, pulling out my phone to snap a picture. But by the time I opened my camera, he was gone.

Still shaking with anger, I looked down at the pink sports bra. In a moment, my outrage transferred from the man and refastened onto my body. "This is your fault," shot through my mind, sending daggers at my chest, shoulders, and bare stomach.

An old memory ricocheted around my brain. An EFY counselor pulls me aside at a dance and points to my shirt. She tells me to go back to the room to change. Her voice is saccharine. She leans in and whispers, "Sister, it's our job to look out for the boys. They can't help it." It was my first time at EFY; I was fourteen.

Another memory. Sitting in Young Women's while the bishop shares a lesson on chastity, his voice is also dripping with honey. "Modesty is so important," he shares, "Boys and men are wired differently than girls."

He pauses and looks around the room at each young woman. "When a young woman dresses immodestly, it is impossible to look away. You can trust me on this; I am a man. I know how it is."

He continued, "If you're dressed in something low cut or revealing, a young man will picture you naked. Really, you might as well *be* naked. It's not a choice young men consciously make; it's simply a reality. As young women, dressing modestly is a commandment from God. This is how you can protect and honor the priesthood."

As the bishop spoke, my hands tightened against my thighs. I resisted the urge to adjust my skirt and ensure it was covering my knees. My mind scanned my body, trying to sense if there was too much skin showing without looking down and admitting default guilt. I was fifteen.

Standing there in the Texas sun, still sweaty from my run, I hated myself. The sports bra, the man in the car, the moment I saw what he was doing—it was the fulfillment of a prophecy. People had tried to warn me about this moment for years, and

I still tempted God. I took my shirt off. I dressed immodestly. I deserved the punishment.

When I crossed paths with that man, and he saw me running, I threw invisible chains around his car. My body entrapped his mind, his free will utterly sapped as he saw me running half naked—no, completely naked—pornographically bouncing up and down. The devil's claws reached out from my body and possessed his mind. I was asking for it, so he had to give it to me.

I felt deeply responsible, and I stopped running without a shirt on for a long time. I wore leggings instead of shorts, even in the heat. When a white car passed, I recoiled and quickly changed my route. If it looked even vaguely familiar, I would snap a photo—just in case. Even though I reported it to the police, nothing ever happened. This was several years ago now; they will never catch him.

In the weeks following that day, I couldn't shake the oppressive guilt. Logically, I could explain the guilt away. Obviously, it wasn't my fault. Obviously, I didn't want this to happen to me. But no matter how many times I tried to drown out the guilt with reason, it always seeped back into my mind. I felt dirty, immoral, and worthless.

Five years after I left the church, the teachings and shame were still bubbling at the surface. Even though I felt free, my mind still wound tightly around the lies. The experience was damaging in many ways, but the most chilling, lasting effect was realizing how much the church still influenced me. I have spent years deconstructing my religious experience. Hours and hours were dedicated to therapy, reading, journaling, and talking with friends. My bucket list seemed complete—smoking, drinking, the normal underwear, taking my name off the roster—you name it, I had done it.

And after all that time and energy, all it took was a sixty-second experience to drag me back to being that little Mormon girl, a child, tugging at my dress and hoping the bishop wasn't picturing me naked. The aura of freedom I constructed around myself was actually a tight, metal cell. I was still trapped in my Mormon shame.

Summer turned to fall, and then it was winter. The jagged edges of the experience were softened by the friction of time. I stopped holding my breath when a white car passed, and I started wearing running shorts again. I even run in a sports bra occasionally. However, if I'm running in a remote area or while it's dark out, I keep myself covered and ignore the heat as well as I can.

While I don't bristle as easily, that day has lived in my mind since. It reminds me I am still Mormon in ways I can't begin to imagine. Time has carried me far away from the days I was active in the church. Sometimes, time deceives us in that way. You may assume 365 days passing is the same as a year's worth of healing. It is not. In the years to come, I am certain I will have countless moments where my heart stops beating, my body shudders, and my soul will be Mormon again.

It may not have anything to do with body shame. There will be a time when I won't be invited to attend my niece's wedding. Maybe a friend will ask me to help her get an abortion. Or a day when my son says, "Oh my god," in front of his grandma. Someone close to me will pass away, and I will have to cope without any promise or hope of seeing them in the Celestial Kingdom.

Any number of emotionally fraught moments will conjure the Mormon Me still living in my brain. No matter how many times I try to make her disappear, she always emerges back out of the shadows. I know I should try and learn to embrace her and to learn from her. I made the very earnest choice to serve a mission, get married in the temple, and bear my testimony on Sunday. No one forced me to do those things, and at the time, I had a powerful, personal conviction that I was making the best choices possible. Mormon me exists in my past, present, and future. While I don't want her to be part of me, she'll always be there.

AUTHENTIC AUTONOMY

As you sit here now, you are finally a free agent. The church's version of free agency is only a cage decorated with lacy, white curtains covering the bars. Considering all the discussion around free agency, the church only assigns one very particular way to live and be. Doctrinally, free agency is to either choose God or choose darkness. That's not free will.

At present, though, you can finally choose whatever you want. There is no longer a proper way to live—no life path set before you. Marry if you want. Have kids if you want. Travel full-time if you want. Pursue your dream of being an artist if you want. Join an ashram. Live off the grid. Get a PhD. All bets are off. Gather all the expectations ever lumped onto you by Mormonism and chuck them off a cliff.

You belong to yourself now, and even if you make mistakes or go down the wrong path, at least the mistakes will be your own. Feel the old edges of who you used to be. When you see the old

Mormon you pop up, examine the artifact. Note the reaction. Ask, "Does this person still exemplify who I want to be?"

In the first few months Jackson and I were married, I was angry constantly. The same series of events would take place over and over again. We would be in Provo, walking around and enjoying a summer evening. As we walked, a woman would pass with jean shorts riding up her hips. Her shoulders would be bare, or her shirt would be cut low across her chest.

Though there was no sign Jackson was checking out anyone, my jealousy would immediately overcome rational thinking. Whether he acted like it or not, I knew he was picturing her naked. As I had been told time and time before: men can't help it. Immodesty was the same as nudity, and I was convinced Jackson was too considerate to tell me what was truly happening in his mind. When a woman walked past us wearing anything I deemed immodest, I felt like I was going to lose it.

Initially, I attempted to hide how upset I was, but after a few months, I finally explained what was bothering me. "All men are like this," I told him, "You can't control yourself. You just don't want to tell me how you really feel!"

He very kindly but firmly responded, "I have control over my mind. I am not picturing anyone naked. I know you can't see in my mind, but please try to trust me."

Trust was elusive. In my twenty-three years on earth, I had never had an open conversation with a man about sex or sexuality. Despite this fact, there was a massive backlog of information to work through. There were years and years of Young Women's lessons and conversations with my mom to deconstruct. Conference talks about pornography and exchanges with bishops about chastity bloomed up in my mind any time there was a sex scene in a movie. *I knew* Jackson was mentally cheating on me, no matter how many times he tried to deny it. I knew he was secretly addicted to porn and watched it constantly. I knew he wanted to have sex with every woman who crossed his path.

A year of marriage finally began to unwind my fears. After three years of marriage, months could pass before I experienced this familiar, irrational jealousy. Jackson and I had countless conversations. I told him the story about my bishop, and told him every man pictures women naked. Jackson told me the bishop was a creep. This rationale had never crossed my mind.

I am eight years into my relationship, and this ugly Mormon beast still raises his head from time to time. In the same way I still feel the echoes of body shame, my distrustful heart prickles at the occasional bikini commercial. Now, if I feel worried about something, Jackson's loving voice enters my mind. The bishop's voice has almost completely disappeared.

Mormonism is a complex mesh to detangle from the brain. The doctrine weaves through so many parts of myself. Even if I can logically step away from a particular belief, my gut convinces me otherwise. Recovering from an all-encompassing, controlling church takes a lifetime. It takes significant work and time to deprogram decades of religious messaging.

Shame and guilt will always permeate my existence, though their influence and strength dissipate over the years. I am getting stronger. I am getting better at detangling myself and my being from the years and years of Mormon me. I am practicing patience and making my voice the loudest in my head.

There is strength in finding yourself amidst all the crowded chatter. Coffee is delicious, and wearing my own underwear is even better. But the permission to think and choose for myself is the best part of leaving the church. Hours and hours of my existence have been spent in prayer, hoping and waiting for the tiniest feeling to urge me left or right down the path of life.

Now, instead of waiting for some flutter in the pit of my stomach, I confidently move forward. As "Invictus," the poem by William Ernest Henley explains, "I am the master of my fate: I am the captain of my soul." I am the God of my world. I am no respecter of persons or gods. On this day, I choose to serve myself and my loved ones. My mistakes belong to me, as do my triumphs.

Life is not what I dreamed of as a kid. These days, when I wake up in the morning, I lace up my shoes and go for a run. Jackson watches our two boys once they wake up and makes them breakfast. He never needs to ask me what our kids like to eat or where to find their socks. He already knows. When I get back from my run, I make our coffee. We sip and chat while my oldest, Eli, plays with Legos at the table. My youngest, West, toddles from toy to toy, occasionally glancing back to make sure his dad and I are where he left us.

Jackson heads to work while I stay home with the kids. During naptime, I work on my book. It's taken me two slow years, but I'm in the editing phase, and it feels triumphant. Once nap time ends, I take the boys out for a bike ride. I wear a tank top and athletic shorts. We stop under an oak tree and sip water in the cool shade. If Eli falls off his bike, he cries and I give him hugs and kisses. I don't lecture him "boys don't cry." Instead, we talk through what happened and how he can be safer next time.

That night, Jackson cooks dinner while I play with the kids. He brings up an interesting article about legalizing psilocybin, and I share a podcast I recently heard on the topic. After the table is set, I pour two glasses of wine, and Eli asks if we can say, "Cheers!" We clink our glasses with his water and toast to the day. Jackson plays *Dark Side of the Moon* while we eat. We discuss meeting friends at a brewery over the weekend. "Let's suggest the one with the play ground. Eli and West will love it!"

I put the kids to bed while Jackson cleans the kitchen after dinner. Once the kids are asleep, we watch *Kill Bill.* We've been working our way through all the Quentin Tarantino films. Jackson's favorite is *Pulp Fiction*, and mine is *Once Upon a Time in Hollywood.*

After the movie ends, we lay in bed and discuss the future. Jackson's business is doing well; hopefully, soon, he'll quit his job and work for himself full-time. He asks for my thoughts on his current website design. We discuss my book and I ask for him to read a chapter and give me feedback. He tells me he's proud of me. I smile and respond, "I'm proud of you, too."

While this day feels typical to me, it's interwoven with moments I never imagined as an active Mormon. And yet, these average, ordinary days are the most magical, beautiful times of my life. My father never cooked us dinner. My Mormon friends rarely have help when cleaning the kitchen. My garments would keep me from wearing a tank top and shorts on a bike ride. From R-rated movies to psychedelic discussions, the discussions between Jackson and me are as vast and open as the expanse of the universe. Nothing is off-limits.

Eli has never heard his dad say, "Boys don't cry," and he's never seen either of us pray. He doesn't know who Jesus Christ is, and every day he sees his father cooking and cleaning and treating his mother with respect. Sometimes, Jackson smokes on our patio. I enjoy an occasional glass of wine with dinner. We are still good stewards of our family. We decide what little pieces compose our day. Every interaction and choice is tinged with love for our children, love for each other, and love for ourselves.

Owning your life is remarkably intoxicating. I hope in reading this book and working through each chapter, you have begun to feel the same way. I hope your new days outside of Mormonism are as unremarkable and simultaneously unexpected as mine. You are doing so well, reader. And I hope if no one in your life is loving you and praising you for making such a difficult, courageous life change, you feel it from me. I am proud of you. I see you and your struggles. If I was sitting there next to you, I would give you a massive hug.

You can do this. You can leave the Mormon church. Leave it behind completely. Root it out of yourself and your heart and your mind. Keep only what serves you, makes you happy, and lifts those around you. For the rest, find it, examine it, learn from it, and then toss it to the ground. The rest of your life is anxiously waiting for you. Go out and live it.

REFLECT AND WRITE

- How does it feel to reach the end of this book? Who have you become as you've deconstructed your Mormon faith?
- What experiences are you most proud of? What do you feel you still need to learn and discover?
- Go back to page 44 and mark your current position on the scale. Have you changed? What has remained the same?
- Which chapters made you the most uncomfortable? Why? Which chapters were the most exhilarating? Why?
- What work do you still need to do as you process leaving the church?

ENDNOTE

You can't start the next chapter of your life if you keep re-reading the last one.

—Unknown

The phrase "Ex-Exmormon" has kicked around the internet for a while. When I first heard it, the term immediately resonated with me. It is the promise that someday you'll be unconditionally free from Mormonism *and* Exmormonism. Mormonism is an obsessive headspace, and the deconstruction and emotional demands of becoming Exmormon can be even more taxing.

I may not yet be at the Ex-Exmormon stage, but I know many people who are. If an old friend who left the church several years ago knocks on my door and I say, "What is wanted?" when I answer—there's a pause before the laugh of recognition. Mormonism is no longer right at the surface, it is an old memory that requires some dusting.

In the initial months of leaving the LDS church, binging podcasts, TikTok, and history books is completely normal. When I first left the church, I wanted to talk about it constantly with everyone I met. Becoming an Exmormon is a phase of intense discovery and renegotiation. But after you process the loss of faith, the world opens even further.

When you break up with someone you've dated for a while, you probably spend some time staring at their social media accounts, asking friends if they've bumped into your ex, and writing in your journal about the relationship. After some time, you start looking outward again, and suddenly your barista or classmate or coworker is looking awfully cute. When I was a teenager, I thought breakups would break me, and now I can hardly remember names.

This is how I view becoming an Ex-Exmormon. The breakup is over; your heart is free, and you are ready to fall deeply in love with a new life, free from your abusive religion. I hope you become so Ex-Exmormon, this book becomes completely irrelevant to you. I see you picking up this book, thumbing through the pages, and letting out a sigh of recognition.

If you are firmly in the Ex-Exmormon phase of your life, don't lose this book in the back of your closet or donate it to the Goodwill void. Here's what I hope you do: hold on to it and keep it safe. Write your Exmormon testimony inside the cover. Wait for the right moment. Inevitably, someone close to you will reach out with some old, familiar words.

You'll open your phone and see the message, "I wanted to reach out to see if you could share more about leaving the church. I've been going through a faith crisis and it's been incredibly hard.

I'm still going to church, but have little to no faith that any of it is true. I'm struggling and I'm not sure what to do."

Save this book for when you get that message, and along with your conversations and the support I am sure you'll offer, ask for their address. Send this book to the next person who needs it. I hope as you drop it in the post, there's a smile on your face. The bad breakup is over, time to fall in love with yourself, your new life, and everything in the world waiting for you.

ABOUT THE AUTHOR

Alyssa Grenfell was raised in a devout Mormon family. She attended Brigham Young University, served a full-time mission, and married in the temple at 23. A year after exiting the church, she moved to New York City and began her faith deconstruction. With her book, *How to Leave the Mormon Church*, she hopes to support and guide those who also choose to leave Mormonism and blaze a new path forward.

Made in United States
North Haven, CT
25 January 2024

47920732R00174